Edmund Booth

❧❧❧

Edmund Booth

DEAF PIONEER

Harry G. Lang

Gallaudet University Press
Washington, D.C.

Gallaudet University Press
Washington, D.C. 20002
http://gupress.gallaudet.edu

Library of Congress Cataloging in Publication Data

Lang, Harry G.
  Edmund Booth : deaf pioneer / Harry G. Lang
     p.   cm.
  Includes bibliographical references and index.
  ISBN 1-56368-273-7 (pbk. : alk. paper)
  1. Booth, Edmund, 1810–1905. 2. Deaf—United States—Biography. I. Title.

HV2534.B64L35   2004
305.9′082′092—dc22
[B]

                                                                    2004043301

The cover photograph of Edmund Booth is from the Booth family album,
courtesy of The Haggin Museum, Stockton, California.

Contents

Preface

EDMUND Booth was a Renaissance man, a farm boy who grew up to distinguish himself as a journalist, educator, and founder of schools and organizations. He stood nearly 6 feet 3 inches tall, wore a long full beard, and weighed more than 210 pounds. He was a brawny adventurer whose life spanned almost the entire nineteenth century—94 years, 7 months, and 5 days. He was also profoundly deaf, as well as blind in one eye, and he possessed "the soul of a pioneer and a spirit restless for freedom and independence."*

Next to Edmund's photograph on the wall of my study is a map of the California Trail. Small pins mark the locations where Edmund camped on his way to California in 1849. Prior to spending five years during the California Gold Rush as a "forty-niner," Edmund had built the first frame house in Anamosa, Iowa. He and his remarkable wife, Mary Ann Walworth Booth, were raising a family in the wilderness during a time when the country was new and much of the land uncharted. There was no white settlement five miles west of their new homestead. One marvels to picture this deaf couple living without fear on the Plains among wildcats and rattlesnakes in often unpredictable weather.

I was indeed excited about being invited by Wilma Spice, the Booths' great-great-granddaughter, to write a biography of Edmund and to highlight the bravery and spirit of Mary Ann on the Iowa frontier. Mary Ann had gone West with her family while Edmund was still teaching at the institution for deaf pupils in Hartford, Connecticut. She played a key supportive role in Edmund's life as he found his niche in journalism and became an "Honored Nestor" of the American Deaf community. An earlier

* *The Silent Worker* 34 (1922): 125.

book, *Edmund Booth (1810–1905), Forty-Niner: The Life Story of a Deaf Pioneer,* first published in 1953, was an important document created from parts of Edmund's life. It was compiled from the journal he kept during his trip on the California Trail; some of his correspondence with Mary Ann; and his autobiographical notes. The present book interprets his life as a whole and includes additional material written by Edmund as well as the reminiscences of his children. Edmund's accomplishments are examined in depth, and Mary Ann's contributions and perspectives are also illuminated. To highlight Edmund's account of the trip across the country during the great California Gold Rush, portions of his journal have been included, some verbatim, others paraphrased to provide a more readable text. The summary of his early and later years has been condensed from Edmund's autobiographical notes written after he was 75 years old. Begun on November 8, 1885, he frequently limited his writing, partly due to a problem with trembling hands, to one or two pages at a time. Urged by his children to persist, he did not complete the writing until after Mary Ann's death in 1898. Combined with the reminiscences of his children, Edmund's reflections provide an enthralling mosaic of the life of a nineteenth-century deaf couple living on the frontier with three hearing children.

❧❦❧

I RECEIVED much help, enthusiasm, and support while preparing this book. Appreciation is due the Haggin Museum in Stockton, California, for granting permission to modify and incorporate materials from *Edmund Booth (1810–1905), Forty-Niner: The Life Story of a Deaf Pioneer.* Susan Benedetti, in particular, deserves special mention for her enthusiastic support of the project, as does Kimberly Bowden for her help with the illustrations. Bertha Finn, one of the editors of the book *Anamosa, 1838–1888. . . . A Reminiscence,* was also instrumental in locating information. Cecilia Hatcher, who, at the time of this writing, lives in a house Edmund Booth built, deserves a note of thanks for keeping her watchful eye out for relevant documents.

In 1997, Jill Porco and John "Vic" Van Cleve from Gallaudet University collaborated on a paper about Edmund and Mary Ann Booth, which

they presented at the International Deaf History conference at Trondheim, Norway. They were kind enough to share their research materials
and their rich perspectives on many aspects of the lives of Mary Ann and
Edmund Booth. Their research played a key role in accelerating the progress of this book and I am deeply appreciative of their help.

Helen Adele Brewer Heckenlaible is one of the great driving forces behind preserving the
memory of Edmund and Mary Ann Booth, her great-grandparents. She celebrated her 100th
birthday in September 2003. In this photograph, she is wearing her Daughters of the American
Revolution ribbon with eighteen gold bars for eighteen Revolutionary War patriot ancestors—
including one of Edmund Booth's grandfathers as well as both of Mary Ann's grandfathers
and one of her great-grandfathers. Courtesy of Charles G. Spice, Jr.

Joan Naturale, Morna Hilderbrand, and Linda Copolla from Rochester Institute of Technology's Wallace Memorial Library; and Sarah Hartwell at Dartmouth College helped me locate many materials. Gary E. Wait, archivist at the American School for the Deaf, supported me throughout the project by looking up information in the records of the school where Booth first was a student and later a teacher. I am indebted to Mark Benjamin for his kind assistance in scanning the photographs and for his patience. Others who provided dialogue, guidance, and support include Kathleen Sullivan Smith, Susan Stevenson Coil, Judy Yaeger Jones, Mickey Jones, Jerry Siders, Ulf Hedberg, Michael Olson, and Ronald Sutcliffe. Lynette Lee Bloom, Barbara LeClere Rowan, and Thomas Edgcomb Booth assisted me in locating materials and information about the Booth family. I am especially indebted to Ivey Pittle Wallace at Gallaudet University Press for her advice, encouragement, and patience as I navigated the intricacies of writing this biographical work.

To my wife, Bonnie Meath-Lang, again much appreciation and love for sharing my mind's eye. We traveled back in history together through our many discussions, this time over the California Trail, five years in the gold mines, and six decades of life in the quaint little town of Anamosa, Iowa. Bonnie's insights have always been cherished; she is a great companion in my various adventures into "Deaf Heritage."

This book is dedicated to Helen Heckenlaible, great-granddaughter of Edmund and Mary Ann Booth; to Helen's daughter, Wilma Spice; and to all of the Booth family descendants for their unfailing generosity of spirit, their material and personal support, and their helpful comments. Most particularly, I could not have written this biography without Wilma's tireless efforts in sharing her heirloom documents and in honoring her family and her own heritage.

Edmund Booth

The Wanderer

Edmund Booth

Wanderer in a distant land.
'Mid scenes all beautiful and grand.
Why sad thine eye?—thy brow in gloom?
Art suffering from a wanderer's doom?
Cheer up, that doom will pass away.
And what is darkness will be day;
Our life by turns is sun and cloud.
The silence deep, the thunder loud;
To give to joy its greater zest.
The heart sometimes demands unrest.

Wanderer! toiling in the mine,
Does one fair spirit on thee shine?
Thy children gather round thy knee.
With shouts and laughter, fond and free?
Of course thy heart will image forth
Such pictures of thy household worth.
Cheer up! that picture shall be real—
Till then let hope thy courage steel;
With heart and soul and honor high.
Bear bravely through thy darkened sky.

Wanderer! on the ocean lone.
Where minds flow free and waters moan.
Or dash tempestuous in their might.
Then sink to rest like day in night.
Art sad?—doth sorrow touch thee sore.
When fades from thought the breakers' roar?
Ah, well! the memory needs to crave
The loved and loving—or the grave.
But cheer thee! transient fate's decree.
Hope on, hope ever is for thee!

Wanderer! when thou turnest back.
Upon the old remembered track.
And seekest with almost dizzied brain.
Those thou has left, nor seekest in vain;
And greetest with a father's heart,
Thy loved ones ne'er again to part,
Keep heart and soul and honor clear—
And all whatever thou holdest dear,
Like peaceful, calm and flowering river.
Shall be to thee a joy forever.

ONE

The Early Years

T H E extraordinary life of Edmund Booth began on a farm in Chicopee, Massachusetts, a town near Springfield, on August 24, 1810. His father, Peter Booth, and mother, Martha Eyre Booth, had four sons and two daughters. The Booth family had originally come from England (their earliest known ancestor, Adam De Booth, was born about 1200 A.D.). Edmund's grandfather, Joseph Booth, was a captain in the American Revolutionary War. Peter Booth's sister (Edmund's aunt), born July 4, 1776, was named Independence Booth, reflecting the importance of the Revolution in Joseph Booth's life. For many years, Edmund's family kept a six-foot-long Revolutionary War flintlock gun, a field officer's hat with feather, and an old sword. As a boy, Edmund had cherished these items as an important part of his family's history. He also treasured a granite Indian hoe that his father had found while plowing the farm in Chicopee.

Martha Eyre's father, who had also come from England, was ruined financially by the Revolutionary War. He became a successful schoolteacher, and Martha's interest in keeping a journal was likely influenced by her father's avid interest in literacy. This passion for writing was passed on to Edmund.

When Edmund was about a year old, his family moved to Long Meadow, Massachusetts, where his father had purchased an interest in a grist mill. Shortly after they moved, a flood broke a dam and the mill was damaged. The grist mill was then sold to new owners. The family moved again, when Edmund was about the age of three or four, into a large two-story house on Iowa Street. Edmund faintly remembered sitting on the floor near the fireplace of this house, watching his mother sewing while his father sat talking with another man. He could not remember ever hearing his father's voice.

During his early years, Edmund was a rather quiet child, often seemingly lost in thought. His mother later told him that while other children in the family would frequently go outside to play, he sat or stood silent. He did not remember ever having sat in his father's lap. His primary recollection of his father was that his hands trembled while he read the newspaper by candlelight. On March 5, 1815, at the age of 42, Edmund's father died of meningitis, then known as *spotted fever*. Edmund's last memory of Peter was the sight of two men placing his father's body in a coffin, and the long funeral procession from the house to the cemetery. His mother held his hand the entire way.[1]

Edmund contracted the same disease three days later. He was about four years old at the time. "Of that sickness of three months duration," he later wrote, "I know nothing whatever beyond what I have been told. Death was expected and my grave clothes were made ready. They tell me my brain was affected and that I was insane [delirious]. I only know that I lost hearing, save a little in the left ear, and the [sight of the] left eye wholly."[2]

Even as a young boy, Edmund believed that "nature was a better physician than the Doctor." Though seriously ill, he cried to his sister Hannah for "flag tops," wild irises that were thought to have medicinal potential. Hannah and a cousin went down the hill and gathered the wildflowers, which he ate. The doctor had just told them to let Edmund have whatever he wanted as he would die anyway.[3]

Edmund surprised them all by recovering from his illness. Over the following months, his mother taught him to read. She began by sitting him on her lap and, while pointing to each letter of the alphabet with a straw from a broom, encouraging him to name each letter, using the little hearing he had left in one ear. When Edmund's mother later sent him to a school, the instructors said they could not teach the young deaf boy. Two teachers, Eunice Cooley and a family cousin, Margaret Booth, could barely hear his voice and were the only ones ever to speak with him because "it required too close proximity of mouth and ear to be convenient or perhaps pleasant." He retained a small amount of residual hearing "until the age of seven or eight, when, with another boy, [he] spent nearly a day sporting in an old pond. The next morning [he] was totally deaf."[4]

Through the next few years, Edmund was free to play, fish, or swim; he sometimes walked the mile to his Uncle David's without informing his mother, who worried about his wanderings. When Edmund was about eleven years old, his mother married Levi Rumrill from Hampton, Massachusetts. Edmund helped his stepfather work in a tobacco field west of the Connecticut River, hoeing rows of tobacco and tying their stalks. He also enjoyed trout fishing in his spare time. When he was twelve, he moved in with his Uncle David, who had a larger farm and needed assistance. David never overworked him or his own sons, for that matter, and the farm was quite prosperous.

The stories of Edmund's youth reflect a good measure of communication with both his stepfather and uncle, although he never learned to read lips well. He reported that he had learned fingerspelling at this time, but he does not reveal who taught him. The Connecticut Asylum for the Education and Instruction of Deaf and Dumb Persons had been established in Hartford in 1817 and was a little more than 20 miles away. Although some of Edmund's neighbors were employed at the school, Edmund apparently did not learn of it until the spring of 1827, when he was sixteen.

> [A] man called and wished to see me. His name was Flavel Goldthwait, son of an old neighbor, and who, with his family, lived a mile or so down street. I was called into the parlor where he was and he began to use the hand alphabet with which I was familiar, and now and then a sign, the language of the deaf. He told me of the Hartford school and that I could go there for an education.[5]

Flavel Goldthwait was a foreman in the cabinet shop of the Asylum. That evening Edmund went home and told his mother about the school. She became interested at once and, in a day or two, discussed it further with David. His uncle was at first opposed to Edmund's going to school, worried that they would not accept him because he could speak. Edmund's mother insisted on giving it a try, and Edmund himself remained persistent, although he was concerned that David needed his help on the farm. He later wrote of his admission to the school,

> Mother did not give up nor rest [until] a letter was written to the governor
> of the state, signed by the clergyman Baxter Dickinson, Mr. Ely, Justice of
> the Peace and two or three others. A reply came from the Secretary of the
> State that the quota of Massachusetts was full and that I should have the
> next vacancy. In the spring following a certificate of admission came from
> the Secretary, and in May 1828, I entered the Hartford School.[6]

The Connecticut Asylum for the Education and Instruction of Deaf and Dumb Persons was chartered in 1816 by the General Assembly of Connecticut. It was the first school of its kind in the country, and it offered an education to deaf children and young adults living in Connecticut and the surrounding states. Up until this time, only a handful of the approximately 6,000 deaf people living in the United States had received formal education. A year after the school opened, "Connecticut" was replaced with "American" in the school's name. The first group of deaf students had also taken issue with the word "Asylum," but the board saw a benefit in keeping the term—they believed it would make it easier to request funds.[7] When Edmund first came to the school in May 1828, the American Asylum had celebrated its first decade under the eminent educators Thomas Hopkins Gallaudet and Laurent Clerc, the first deaf teacher in the United States.

Distinguished visitors to the Hartford school during its early years included President James Monroe and Margaret Hall, the wife of Captain Basil Hall of the Royal Navy and daughter of Sir John Hunter, consul general in Spain. Many spoke favorably of the quality of the education they observed. In 1827, Hall accompanied her husband to North America to investigate prisons, asylums, and schools. She described in some detail her observations of the American Asylum, noting that four of the nine teachers were deaf and that Gallaudet and Clerc had both married deaf women. Hall had visited the school on the last day of vacation so there were no classes that day, but most of the pupils had returned. She wrote that "a more cheerful or more intelligent looking group I never saw."

Gallaudet brought three of the girls and two boys into a room to give Hall a demonstration, which she described as follows:

> There was no trick, nothing got up in the exhibition . . . .We wrote down questions on the slate and they answered them, sometimes off hand, at other times they required a little reflection. We then wrote a word, an adjective, or adverb, or any part of speech we chose which they brought in in [sic] a sentence and always so as to show that they understood the meaning perfectly. There was generally a great deal of imagination in the form of their replies. The system of signs is very quick. They use the alphabet very little and entirely with one hand.[8]

Clerc, Gallaudet, and their colleagues were indeed inspirational teachers who developed in their students a passion for the humanities as well as functional literacy. Among their scholars were George Henry Loring and Wilson Whiton, two of the first seven pupils, who were educated well enough to become instructors. Loring was extremely fond of poetry and literature. Levi Backus, also one of the first pupils, later took up journalism as a career and became America's first deaf editor, establishing a weekly newspaper in Canajoharie, New York.

RAILROADS having yet to be built in the Northeast, Edmund and his older brother Charles made the 22-mile trip to Hartford by stagecoach. When they arrived,

> The coach stopped at the front door and we emerged therefrom. A few small boys came around with curious looks, the nearest, with bright eager face and quick eyes scanned me from head to foot, glanced at Charles who was talking and attending to baggage, motioned to the next nearest boy, then to me, and said I was a *new pupil*. I did not understand then, but guessed and remembered these simple signs. We entered the hall, and in a few minutes Mr. Gallaudet, the Principal, came. He talked with Charles, wrote down some notes, made a few signs to me to ascertain if I understood, and I did not, and left. Charles and I went into the boys' and, next, the girls' study or sitting rooms. It was all new to me and to Charles it was amusing, the innumerable motions of hands and arms. After dinner he left and I was among strangers but knew I was at home.[9]

"Home" for Edmund, as for many deaf children then and now, was a place where he could be with others who understood the isolation of being the only deaf person in a hearing family. It was a place where he could both communicate comfortably with others and develop his mind. Gallaudet taught the first or highest class in the school, and Clerc taught the second. Edmund began in the third class, which was taught by William W. Turner. He learned well and moved into Clerc's class after about two-and-a-half years. Edmund appreciated his education in general, although he later reflected on how language was taught without appropriate emphasis on thinking skills.

> The mode of teaching was by natural signs and sentences dictated by word signs. The idea, of all except Clerc, seemed to be that the deaf of all ages, from 14 to 30, should learn language as hearing babies learned, the bringing out and forward the verbal memory but not the reasoning faculties. It was, in fact, a parrot system. Phrenology, a division of faculties, in that day was [unknown], save to a very few and not at all among teachers. . . . In Clerc's class I saw for the first time that written language has its laws. Still even he did not make these laws clear.[10]

Edmund was impressed with Gallaudet's ability to read the expressions on his students' faces. During their first encounter outside the school, Gallaudet had challenged him with the word *accumulate,* and he knew immediately that it was a word with which the young deaf boy was not familiar. Edmund described Gallaudet as

> a man of quick-temper, never in a passion, and who was governed by love, reason and earnest persuasion. He was not born to command but to persuade, and yet to be always in the right. This lack of self-assertion left teachers to act much as they pleased. . . . Genuine and kindly benevolence, active mentality in the perceptive and reflective sense, sincere friendship, and a love of humor where humor was not inappropriate, these were his leading characteristics. . . .
>
> Now and then, but rarely, I have seen his face deeply saddened and felt

The American Asylum for the Education and Instruction of Deaf and Dumb Persons (now the American School for the Deaf) in Hartford, Connecticut, in the 1830s, the time when Edmund Booth was a student. Courtesy of American School for the Deaf. From *The American Magazine of Useful and Entertaining Knowledge* 1:4 (December 1834).

an unexpressed sympathy for him as it led me to think over the problems of life.[11]

Edmund himself was a young man destined to set high ideals throughout his life. He took one such step on July 6, 1829, a little more than a year after his arrival at the American Asylum, when he joined several students in organizing a school temperance society, whose members promised "to abstain entirely, and at all times, during life, from the use of ardent spirits," except for medicinal purposes.[12] Edmund's name was second on the charter. Two years later, with William Willard and a dozen other students, he discussed the possibility of one day joining together to purchase land in the West with the hope that they would further enjoy their friend-ships as deaf people who shared unique experiences and a common sign language. "Time went on," Booth later reflected, "and we all found our-selves compelled to attend to the stern realities of life—procuring a self-support—before we could attend to carrying out what . . . Willard [later] called our Don Quixotic scheme"[13] This was not the last time Edmund would be involved in a discussion about the establishment of a deaf state in the Western United States. He would address these same concerns with great detail in letters he wrote to the *American Annals of the Deaf and Dumb* in the 1850s.

The annual reports of the directors of the American Asylum regularly included "Specimens of Original and Uncorrected Compositions" of the young scholars. Edmund's compositions usually were preceded by a com-ment that "he lost his hearing partially at four and entirely at eight years of age, and though he retained the knowledge of many words in our lan-guage when he joined the school, was quite unable to write connect-edly."[14] Edmund's teachers perhaps wrote comments like this to contrast the grammar in his compositions with those of his peers who never had heard spoken language.

The content of Edmund's writings reflected his quality education and early passion for reading. In 1829, he wrote an account of the invasion of Greece by the Persians, as signed by a fellow student. In 1830, he penned a perceptive essay on astronomy. "Among almost every uncivilized na-tion," he wrote, "the heavenly bodies are worshipped as gods, or some respect is paid to them as beings of a superior order, who have power over the fate of man. It requires only a general and liberal diffusion of religion and knowledge to free a people from such superstitious notions and raise them to the standard of civilization."[15]

The following year the school's annual report included a creative dia-logue between a Greek patriot and an educated deaf man from the United States, in which they discussed liberty, human rights, and the fruits of education of deaf people. Edmund was the precocious young author. In 1832, his composition examining the present state of European govern-ments also was selected for inclusion in the school's annual report. In

1833, he wrote on education in the United States and stressed the need for early stimulation of children's minds. And, in 1834, he submitted a soliloquy in the voice of Napoleon Bonaparte on his voyage to exile in St. Helena.

Edmund also began to dabble in poetry. One of his earliest poems was included in the *Seventeenth Report of the American Asylum*. Written on April 1, 1833, "To No One But Myself," reflects typical nineteenth-century conventions such as rhyme and sentimentality.

> Come, the day is fair,
> The bees are humming in the air,
> The sun is laving in the lake,
> The fishes sporting near the brake;
> So come, and drink the balmy breeze
> By soft gales wafted from the trees.
>
> The lake is like an angel's path,
> And spotted like a flowery heath
> With islands lovely as itself;
> No rock or mountain-crag or delf
> But smiles upon the glassy wave
> Or lies contented in its grave.
>
> So come—O! come and let us go,
> The day is still—the wind is low
> There's nothing to disturb or break
> The drowsy woods—or sleeping lake.
> The spell of Nature's loveliness
> Hath power to wrap the soul in bliss.
>
> The boat is waiting on the shore
> And ready hangs the lightsome oar;
> T'will glitter as we move along
> And that shall be our only song,
> Save where some wild bird's mood subdued
> Gives echo to the solitude.[16]

AMONG the instructors at the Asylum was Frederick Augustus Porter Barnard, a Yale graduate whose own deafness had increased over the years.[17] When Barnard fell ill and took a leave of absence, Edmund was invited to teach his Classics class, which included four girls and eleven boys. One of his pupils, Mary Ann Walworth, had also become deaf at the age of four from spotted fever. Short, with light brown hair and hazel eyes, Mary Ann was very expressive and left an impression on her young teacher. She had few memories of sounds or voices, but one of the few things she did remember from her early years was learning to recite, "Mary Had a Little Lamb."

Mary Ann was a descendent of William Walworth, who had come to New London Colony (Connecticut) in 1689 from London. In 1690, he married a young Englishwoman, Mary Seaton, an orphan who had come to New London on the same ship. William died after thirteen years in the colony, leaving Mary a widow with seven children. She eventually settled in Canaan, New Hampshire, where her great-grandson George Walworth was born in 1779. In 1807, George, a town selectman, married Philura Jones. Mary Ann Walworth was born to George and Philura on February 23, 1817, in Canaan. She was the fifth of nine children. In 1831, at the age of fourteen, she left home to attend the American Asylum.[18]

IN THE fall of 1831, Edmund became a full-time instructor, replacing George Henry Loring, who had returned to his home in Boston. Barnard had come back to teach his class, so Edmund received a class of his own. Now 21 years old, he was a towering figure—about 6 feet 3 inches tall and as physically strong as he was mentally sharp. His years of farming gave him the rugged features, imposing stature, and musculature that projected an air of authority far beyond his age.

Edmund found teaching to be intellectually stimulating. In addition to interacting with his well-educated colleagues, several of whom had graduated from Yale College, Edmund had the opportunity to meet many of the famous visitors to the school, including Speaker of the House Henry Clay, President Andrew Jackson, and Senator Daniel Webster. But, this period of opportunity also was a time of grief for Edmund. His brother

William, a stonecutter, died on March 5, 1833. His brother Danforth Charles died at the age of 27 on December 27, 1834. Booth's mother and stepfather moved to Bolton, New York, selling many of the family possessions, including the Indian hoe and flintlock rifle. "I never read J. [Fenimore] Cooper's Leather Stocking Tales and 'la longue carbine' without thinking of that long gun sold with such indifference," he reminisced later.[19]

As an instructor, Edmund was both respected and challenged by his hearing colleagues. One day, Lewis Weld, Gallaudet's successor as principal of the Asylum, stormed into Edmund's classroom with a copy of British writer Harriet Martineau's essay, "Letter to the Deaf." Martineau, who began to lose her hearing at the age of twelve, was quite deaf by 1834 when she published her "Letter" in *Tait's Edinburgh Magazine*. In that piece, she compared her deafness to that of a friend who had been deafened at a much younger age. In discussing the challenges and sacrifices associated with deafness, she was somewhat derogatory toward other deaf people. Weld accused Martineau of slandering the entire Deaf community and encouraged Edmund to write an article in reply. But Edmund had already read Martineau's work and viewed it with a more detached irony.

> Miss Martineau told the truth. Of this I was satisfied from the first. But she did not go far enough, and tell the whole truth. She should have included in her sweeping charge of "childishness" and frivolity the entire hearing community also. Of course there are exceptions in both the deaf and the hearing class. They are both the same, the only difference being that one class has one avenue to knowledge closed.[20]

In December 1834, Edmund and two deaf pupils—Joseph Holmes from Charleston, South Carolina, and Thomas S. Perkins of New London, Connecticut—accompanied Weld to South Carolina and Georgia to meet with legislators to advocate that these states send their deaf children to Hartford; neither state had yet established its own school. After the initial meetings in South Carolina, Weld wrote to the president of the Directors of the American Asylum that Edmund "did all that it was reasonable of an intelligent man" [and that] two days later the Legislative Committees made a joint report in the form of a bill "to provide for the education of [deaf] children of this state." Within a week, on December 13, Governor Wilson Lumpkin of Georgia had also received them "with marked affability and kindness, and expressed himself much gratified that we had come."[21]

Weld, Booth, and the two pupils also provided several exhibitions after Christmas. During the demonstrations, Weld would call upon the audience to give quotations or sentences. These were conveyed by signs alone, and Edmund would then go to the blackboard to write them out. The object of the exhibitions was to show the audience that sign language was nearly as rapid a vehicle for communication as spoken language, and that the ideas conveyed in sign language were exactly the same as those conveyed by speech. On one occasion, however, a member of the North Carolina state legislature suggested a challenging verse of poetry for interpretation that was not familiar to most people in the room. Weld signed the verse as carefully as he could, but Edmund was at his wit's end. Then, as he found many times throughout his life, his literacy paid off. He remembered having read the verse and wrote it on the board confidently. It was a moment of glory for the American Asylum.

Not long after his return to the Asylum, however, Edmund became disillusioned by the poor salary he received.

> I began teaching on the old established salary for those who had been pupils. . . . $250 a year and was told that paying more would cause dissatisfaction in the [other deaf teachers]. The sum was barely enough to live on and all of us ran into debt. Board, and its attendants, fuel, lights, washing and traveling expenses more than took up the amount. It worked like the policy of keeping men by compelling them to live on today and the earnings of tomorrow. It was dishonest and my mistake was in accepting the position under the circumstances.[22]

Although Clerc was earning $1,300 per year, most of the other deaf teachers, particularly those not married, were being paid less than half this amount. The contractual agreements called for an annual increase of $100 until salaries reached $550 and then another $50 per year was added. This increase was, however, still inadequate and several deaf teachers resigned. In 1834, Weld urged the executive committee to increase Edmund's salary.

Not all of the teachers shared Weld's view. William W. Turner, who had begun teaching at the school in 1821, was, like Weld, a graduate of Yale, but he was much more paternalistic toward the deaf pupils. Collins Stone, who started in 1833, also characterized the pupils as generally "helpless" and "dependent," and sometimes resorted to even more pre-Enlightenment characterizations.[23] Consequently, nothing was done to satisfy the salary issue over subsequent years. Edmund and the other deaf teachers were told they should not expect much, if any, salary increase, especially because they had been educated by charity. This was "too shallow" an explanation for Edmund. Pay also appeared to depend on other factors, including training and length of service. Edmund felt that "was in accordance with the limited vision of the time," and so he resigned at the close of the 1839 winter term.[24]

Edmund Booth had decided that it was time to leave "home."

TWO

Journey to Iowa

❧❦❧

IN MAY 1839, Edmund left Hartford, Connecticut, for Iowa. His motives were not purely economic. Mary Ann Walworth, the young deaf woman who had charmed him, was now living with her family in the wilderness there. Unfortunately, little is known about the courtship of Edmund and Mary Ann. The affection between them presumably blossomed while Mary Ann was Edmund's student and through correspondence now lost.

In addition to his romance with Mary Ann and the poor salary at the Asylum, Edmund also had health reasons for leaving Hartford. An attack of pneumonia had left him with a desire to be outdoors and active. He was ready for a new chapter in his life. As he reflected,

> [I was] glad to be free and my own master. The world was open to me and the West was bound only by the Pacific. I spent some weeks in Springfield and Suffield where parents and brother Henry resided, sister Hannah at Springfield. They all disapproved of my intention of going west. . . . I had my own views and was weary of being under others whose ideas never extended beyond their own wants, wishes and immediate surroundings.[1]

Edmund's adventurous sixteen-day trip to Iowa began on a regular stagecoach. Traveling through the night and nearly all the next day, he stopped at the Eagle Tavern in Albany, New York, for a few hours and then boarded a train. After arriving in Syracuse, he learned he had a choice of traveling by stage or by canal to Oswego, New York, on Lake Ontario. He chose the latter in order to see this Great Lake, mentioned in James Fenimore Cooper's "Hawkeye" tales. Perhaps this character, the scout

14

trained by the Iroquois, was an inspiration for the well-read deaf pioneer setting out on his own adventure. He had his own solitude and silence and, like Hawkeye, he was resourceful and fearless.

From Oswego Edmund took a steamer to Lewiston, New York, at the mouth of the Niagara River. On the American side of the river, he left the boat and climbed a steep bank, where a train of several coaches was waiting. The train stopped at Niagara Falls, and since another train was starting for Buffalo that afternoon, Edmund took advantage of the available time to be a tourist.

With limited railroad service operating from Albany to Syracuse and from Lockport to Buffalo, Frink and Walker's "mud wagons," as the mail stagecoaches of this western section were called, constituted the only sure means of transport westward. Edmund later wrote that "the old settlers remember the Frink & Walker 4-horse coaches with their big rocking beds; the lofty throne on which the kingly driver was perched in front of the big boot, behind which the boys dearly loved to steal a ride."[2]

Next came a pleasant five-day lake voyage, with brief stops at Detroit and Milwaukee. When Edmund arrived in Chicago, which had been incorporated in 1833, he found a "straggling town" of about 350 people, and no more than 20 frame buildings. Entering one of the stores, he saw an Indian, "painted and standing motionless like a statue, stern looking and leaning against a pile of goods." He noted that town lots were cheap, as low as $75 each.[3] His next stop was Galena, which he reached by a Frink and Walker's mud wagon. The town appeared to be wealthier than Chicago, with regular streets and a larger population. Edmund went into the *Gazette* newspaper office, bought some papers, and mailed them to his sister Hannah in Massachusetts. While he was in the post office, he experienced a fascinating and frightening case of mistaken identity.

> At the post office, as I delivered the papers, the two young men in attendance looked at me sternly or suspiciously as I thought. Supposed it was perhaps some revelation of western manners and gave it no further attention. Had learned that no stage would leave for Dubuque till next day. . . . Returned to the hotel for dinner. Found the piazza filled with a crowd, all standing and gazing at me as though they thought me an ogre or some

other monster. . . . Found dinner was nearly over. Took a seat at the table. The landlord placed before me what was wanted, and I began to eat. Soon a big, burly man entered, stood by my side and spoke orally. I made the usual sign of want of hearing and went on with my dinner. By this time a crowd was standing around in front. A minute or two passed thus and then the burly looking fellow beside me (I suppose he had been speaking and getting no answer or notice in return) tossed a handbill by my plate. It described a murderer in Ohio and tallied almost with my appearance, tall, one eye, *black* hair, mine was light. . . .

I finished dinner and the man asked me, in writing, writing for the first time, if I would allow my baggage to be examined. This caused me to laugh outright for it told me the [suspicion] was more than I had thought it. I arose, beckoned to the bully, a doctor. . . . He followed, some of the crowd also, upstairs to my room. The landlord . . . came in also and sat quietly as though regretting the affair. I pulled forward a couple of trunks and handed my bunch of keys to the doctor. He spoke and I paid no attention. Then he motioned to the trunks and I understood and laid them open, also a carpet bag. One of the trunks was full of books.

Doctor did nothing, so I opened two or three and showed my name and former residences. He took one, Byron, opened on his lap and said something to the crowd. Clothing also with my name. Also on the brass handle of my umbrella. Crowd began to thin out again. . . . The doctor reflected a moment, jumped up and went out. The landlord then wrote that it was all the work of the post office clerks, and asked me to pass over it as a mistake. I may add my name did not correspond with that in the hand bill and that, meeting the doctor afterwards, I told him my hair was not *Black*. His reply was, "Hair can be colored."[4]

The next day Edmund joined about a half dozen men in a stagecoach carrying the mails, and they traveled until dusk, when they reached the Mississippi River opposite Dubuque, Iowa. Dubuque was then a true frontier outpost. It was mid-August 1839.

There was a sort of shanty made of boards nailed perpendicular; open door, no windows or fire place and no sign of being inhabited. The men sent a hail cross, and after a half hour a large skiff came over rowed by one man.

We all entered with the mail bags, and arrived in Dubuque. . . . we stopped at Tim Fanning's . . . tavern. Tim was a tall, lanky, good natured Irishman. His was the only hotel in the town. Being a double log cabin, that is, twice the usual length, and two stories high, it had sufficient accommodations for the travel of that day.[5]

Though Edmund's speech could be understood by others, writing and gesturing seemed to be his primary means of communicating with people he met on the journey to Iowa. In the morning, Edmund asked Fanning if he knew of George H. Walworth, Mary Ann's elder brother, whom he had met in Hartford. Fanning directed Edmund to Timothy Davis, a lawyer from Missouri, whose office was a small shanty. Davis was Walworth's partner.

Edmund was surprised to learn that Mary Ann's family was now located at the "Buffalo Forks" of the Wapsipinicon River, 40 miles southwest of Dubuque. Walworth was building mills there. The letters Edmund had received from the Walworths were always dated Dubuque, and Edmund was dejected to find out that there was still another leg to his journey into the wilderness. Davis, however, was a kind man and offered him the use of a horse he wished to send to Walworth. Later that day Davis came to Fanning's hotel and informed Edmund that two men would be starting for Iowa City the next morning by way of the Buffalo Forks. He was invited to accompany them.

Edmund arrived at Davis's office early in the morning and met the two men mounted on ponies, apparently not much larger than donkeys. Davis's son had a horse saddled and ready for him. The road was only a wagon track through the grass and alongside was a single plowed furrow. Every mile or so there was a mound of sod about four-feet high.

One of Edmund's fellow travelers was a Dubuque merchant named Bartlett. The other man was a blacksmith. Their ponies went at a slow trot while Edmund's large horse took longer steps. Edmund thus felt compelled to walk the horse, but he soon fell behind. He then would mount the horse and put it into a trot until he caught up with his companions. This push-me-pull-you strategy continued until about noon when the trio came to a log dwelling. Edmund saw a small garden and a woman in the house. He and his two companions each paid her a half-dollar for dinner, after which they traveled two miles to the north fork of the Maquoketa River. Here, they found a new frame hotel nearly finished and another house owned by a man named De Long from Kentucky. These and the log house where they took dinner were the only signs of civilization Edmund had seen since leaving Dubuque that morning. Throughout the trip the road never changed—a wagon track through the grass, a furrow, and the sod mounds on the left.

As evening arrived, they entered a timber belt. After what seemed a mile through the timber, the light from a log cabin burst into view through the openings and they knew they were near human habitation. The ranch, on the South Fork of the Maquoketa River, belonged to Daniel Varvell. After dismounting his horse and entering the house, Edmund saw more than a dozen men seated around the room. They were employed by the government to lay out the military road. Supper consisted of wheat bread, fried ham and eggs, and coffee. An hour or so of talk followed, after which Varvell took a lantern and led the way up a ladder to the stable loft. Edmund and the two men spread their saddle blankets on the hay, the horses feeding below, and "slept the sleep of the just."[6]

Leaving Varvell's ranch the next morning, they forded a stream about two or three feet deep at the South Fork of the Maquoketa, and resumed their way southwest. About noon, they passed the first plowed prairie they had encountered on their 40-mile route. They crossed a hill and saw a tall, heavy man coming up the road. Edmund's hearing companions stopped and questioned him. Edmund was some distance behind and they motioned to him to turn off to the right where the road forked. They did not accompany him, as they were headed for Iowa City to attend the first sale of town lots. Edmund wrote of this final short leg of his journey:

> Turning my horse into the road on the right I rode through the low bushes . . . and kept on, whither I could only guess. . . . Saw on the right of the road a piece of four or five acres broken by the plow . . . and unfenced. . . .

Further on . . . descried a log cabin in the distance about a mile. . . . Along my left was the Buffalo Creek. Nearing the cabin I turned the horse's head to the south side but he seemed to insist going on the north. Let him have his way and stopped in front of the only door to the house.[7]

Edumund had arrived at the Walworth homestead, it was August 18, 1839. He saw Emily Walworth, Mary Ann's younger sister, in the house. Emily recognized him, ran out, shook hands, then went around the corner and beckoned him to follow. There, at last, he saw Mary Ann sitting in a carriage, reading.[8]

LIKE Edmund, Mary Ann was an avid reader. Before she was four years old, her father had her reading passages from the family Bible when the Congregational minister of Canaan came to visit their home. At a public exhibition around the same age, she was lifted onto a platform where she recited a poem to the crowd. Mary Ann's adventurous spirit and independence were evident from childhood, when she and her brothers and sisters were responsible for driving a half dozen cows to and from a distant pasture. Emily and Clark were at times afraid to enter the heavy timber on either side of the pasture. They feared a bear or "spook" might attack them at any moment.

Ascending the hill [Emily] was surprised and overjoyed at seeing one of the cows quietly meandering homeward. "I thank you, Betty," she said to herself from the bottom of her heart. Then another cow came to view. "Oh, Rosie, how I thank you too." And presently, one after another, appeared the rest of them, each the unconscious recipient of copious exclamations of increasing surprise and gratitude from Emily, until, last of all, Mary Ann . . . came trudging along, serenely oblivious of either pale-visaged spook or consuming bear. That was a youthful sample of [Mary Ann's] fearlessness and independent spirit.[9]

The Walworths had moved to the Iowa wilderness in the spring of 1839, when the population of the entire county was less than 400. Courage ran in the family blood. Mary Ann's grandfather, Jehu Jones, had served in the Revolutionary Army. More recently, in 1837, Mary Ann's brother George helped fight a proslavery mob in Alton, Illinois. Freedom of speech and independence for all people dominated the family's political views.

Mary Ann's mother, Philura, was an extremely energetic woman. She would wake up regularly at 4:00 a.m., take her Bible and hymn book to a nearby grove, and read for an hour. She would then return to the house for her morning duties and afterwards she would sit down with Caroline, Mary Ann's youngest sister, and have her commit to memory the verses of Scripture. When Philura's friends came to visit, often for several weeks at a time, they would make coats, vests, and pants.

In her childhood, Mary Ann learned to sew and to spin. At school she learned needlework in addition to her academic studies. Over time, she had become a talented seamstress and embroiderer. Unable to enjoy comfortable communication with her family, however, Mary Ann filled many silent days with reading. But this fearless deaf woman also possessed the ability to make repairs around the family's home. She was more than ready for a pioneering life, and Edmund was delighted to be with her again.

THREE

Anamosa

AFTER visiting with Mary Ann at her home, Edmund stopped at the area known as "the Buffalo Forks mills." A group of men were on a break, saw him approach, and came up to greet him. Edmund was given "an old friend's welcome" from Mary Ann's brothers, George, Caleb Clark and John Denison Walworth, further indication that he had gotten to know the Walworth family during his courtship with Mary Ann in the East. He had reached the end of his journey with only $5 in his pocket and $70 in Mobley's Bank in Dubuque. "[M]y first object was some kind of work," he wrote. "Having passed my boyhood on a farm I had no fears regarding success."[1]

Construction on the new mills on the Wapsipinicon River began in July 1839, only two years after the first white settlers had arrived in the area now known as Fisherville, just west of Anamosa. Timothy Davis, Gideon H. Ford, and George H. Walworth owned the mills, but their partnership was known as "Davis and Ford." Walworth withheld his name from the business while he straightened out some previous financial losses. By settler's law, Davis and Ford owned the land that was later named Anamosa. The company employed eighteen men, who were building a dam and sawmill, and the Walworth sisters, who took care of the housework, cooking, and washing. Some of the men had families living on the prairies. When George H. Walworth brought his sisters Mary Ann and Emily from Illinois in the spring of 1839, he also invited a skilled deaf carpenter, Lewis N. Perkins, to help at the mills. Perkins, a former pupil at the American Asylum, was also a friend of Edmund's. Since Perkins and Edmund had learned carpentry at the school, they took responsibility for shingling the new buildings. Edmund agreed to work for $.75 per day, including board.

Buffalo Forks was the only sawmill in the region. Once it began operation on the new dam, locals started bringing in logs and carrying boards home. Later that year, Calvin C. Reed built the first grist mill.

Soon after his arrival, Edmund wrote to his family back East and described the Iowa frontier. Although they had argued against his heading west originally, he must have painted an inviting picture because they agreed to join him there before the following spring. By June 1840, Edmund's brother Henry; his sister Hannah and her husband, Colonel David Wood; their two sons, Charles Danforth and William; and Edmund's mother, now 70 years old, had arrived from Springfield, Massachusetts.

Edmund quickly established his leadership as a frontiersman in the Iowa Territory. During his first year there, he was elected county recorder for a two-year term. He was reelected twice. In the middle of his third term the law was changed, uniting the offices of recorder and treasurer. He was nominated for this position, but he declined it. He also acted as a deputy postmaster for six months. The small compensation—$6 in six months and the recorder's fees—enabled him to purchase 40 acres of land.

By 1840, the county had about 475 people. "The log house at the mills was too limited for convenience," Edmund wrote, "and Col. Wood and I soon agreed to build on what is now Anamosa." A portion of land had been staked into lots for a town and George H. Walworth offered a choice of lots free to Edmund if he built on it. "We did so, getting the lumber at the mills and it was the first house built in Anamosa, and the first frame house in the [region]."[2]

One day in June, Lewis Perkins was helping Edmund dig the cellar for the frame house when Sheriff Hugh Bowen, the first settler in the county, stopped by to collect information for the Census of 1840. Bowen duly noted in the records that the two men were "deaf-mutes."

Months later, Edmund received a copy of the *Hartford Courant* in which he was appalled to read that Mary Ann, Perkins, and himself were listed in the Census records "and for the information of the coming ages

down to the end of time, . . . as 'deaf, dumb, blind, idiotic, insane, colored.' I pause for breath!"[3] For the former schoolmaster who had distinguished himself in writing and language study, this categorization was
both shockingly offensive and stupidly inaccurate.

ॐ∫ई৯

THE long love affair that began as a teacher-student attraction blossomed
on the frontier, and within a year of Edmund's arrival in Iowa, he and
Mary Ann decided to marry. In order to obtain a marriage permit, Edmund had to travel by horseback to Edinburg to see the Clerk of Commis-
sioner's Court, William Hutton. Hutton was not home, and Edmund
learned through queries that he was cradling wheat several miles north of
Cascade in Dubuque County. When he finally located Hutton, neither
had a pen or pencil or paper, but Hutton was willing to return to Cascade
to complete the permit, and Edmund rode home a happy man.

Edmund and Mary Ann were married on Sunday, July 26, 1840, in
their new house. The wedding party included Edmund's mother; brother
Henry and his wife Lucy; sister Hannah, her husband Colonel David
Wood, and their two sons, Charles Danforth and William; Gideon H.
Ford; John Denison Walworth and Emily Walworth, brother and sister of
the bride; and John G. Joslin, the justice of the peace who performed
the ceremony. Mary Ann's brother George was at Burlington attending a
session of the Territorial Legislature, of which he was a member. Her other
brother, Clark, apparently would not attend the wedding in his buckskin
dress; he left the day before the wedding for Iowa City with a load of
lumber. Edmund mused that

> He [Clark] was not philosopher enough to know that dress, if only decent,
> was of small moment on the frontier, and we were emphatically on the fron-
> tier, there being no known white settlement five miles west of us. . . . His
> entire suit was a deer skin coat, vest and pantaloons and all comparatively
> new and clean. The bride expectant had previously objected to the squire
> (Joslin) wearing deer skin clothes. This put it into Clark's head to run away.
> Joslin, however, came well dressed in store clothes, having borrowed a [suit]

Edmund Booth traveled on horseback to Cascade, Iowa, to obtain a wedding permit for his marriage to Mary Ann Walworth. The permit was signed on July 25, 1840, and the wedding performed on July 26 by Justice of the Peace John G. Joslin. The Booth wedding was the first on record for Jones County, Iowa. Courtesy of the Jones County Genealogical Society.

of his son, Dr. Clark Joslin. On the occasion the bride borrowed a pair of pantaloons of me to give her brother Denison a decent appearance.[4]

When the time came for the wedding ceremony, Joslin, who had never performed a wedding, discovered he had no code or manual prescribing the proper ceremonial words. Edmund's literacy paid off again. He was ready for this emergency. He handed Joslin a newspaper report of the recent marriage of Queen Victoria to Prince Albert. This article contained the ceremonial form used at the royal wedding. Joslin agreed that a form good enough for a royal pair was good enough for the Booths. He pointed out the necessary passages in the newspaper account to which Edmund and Mary Ann had to assent. They merely nodded their responses and the ceremony was over.

Shortly after the wedding, Edmund and his brother-in-law Colonel Wood set about digging a well not far from the Booth's framed house. After going down about 30 feet and finding solid rock, they dug 5 feet into the rock, tried to blast it, and failed. The land all around belonged to the mill company and was too rough for a farm. Consequently, Edmund decided to acquire farmland near his brother Henry.[5] Edmund worked for Henry to earn enough money to start his own farm. He bought a yoke of oxen for $60 and then hired a man to clear 10 acres at $2.50 per acre. The following winter he cut and split the rails and hauled them off the land. During that same winter Colonel Wood died of liver problems, leaving Edmund's sister with two children to raise alone. Hannah then married Gideon Ford and Edmund and Mary Ann sold their frame dwelling to the newlyweds, who moved the entire house to the town and turned it into the Wapsipinicon Hotel.

Edmund built a log cabin on his new land south of Reed's creek, a brook that was never dry. In the spring of 1841, he bought a cast-iron plow to prepare the ground for planting corn and raised a very heavy crop. Edmund then tore down the cabin, hauled the logs to a lot he had purchased from their neighbor, Clement Russell, and reassembled the house at the new location. In this log cabin, Thomas Eyre Booth was born on February 11, 1842. That spring and summer, Edmund and Mary Ann continued to farm using a new steel plow, which required only one-fourth the labor of the old cast-iron implement.

EDMUND Booth played a key role in naming the emerging town of Anamosa. One day in the summer of 1842, while he was visiting his sister Hannah and her husband Gideon Ford at the Wapsipincon Hotel, an Indian family stopped by on its way westward. "When we asked the mother the name of her daughter," Edmund explained, "the latter laughed the pleasant, half-bashful laugh of a young girl, showing that she understood the question, but did not speak." Her parents explained that her name was "Anamosa," which meant "White Fawn."[6] The name stuck with Edmund. The area had been called Dartmouth since the early 1840s. When Iowa became a state in 1846, R. J. Cleaveland renamed the area Lexington after the Massachusetts town from which he had come. In 1847, the town post office opened. The government believed Lexington to be too common, and so Edmund offered the name Anamosa. The Board of County Commissioners accepted his suggestion, and the town was officially named Anamosa in 1848.[7] Of the 27 names appearing on the petition to rename the town, 3 were deaf settlers—Edmund Booth, Benjamin Clough, and Lewis Perkins.

࿐࿐

IN THE late autumn of 1843, Mary Ann's father came up from Round Prairie in Bond County, Illinois, with a horse and buggy. Edmund described her father's request that Mary Ann accompany him home for a visit as "urgent," but he did not explain why. It is possible that both George and Philura needed some family support. George was about 62-years-old and Philura was 53, so Mary Ann likely felt a need to provide them with some attention and assistance. It had been four years since they had seen each other.

Edmund was very concerned about the trip. Thomas was not yet two years old and Bond County was about 300 miles away. The Mississippi River was frozen and, without a railroad, the only course of travel was through Iowa City, which consisted of just a few buildings along the three sides of the square and a stone state house.

The day Mary Ann and Thomas left, Edmund had a fever and he suffered with chills for the next four nights. He went to Dubuque during the first week of December to seek help from a mesmerist named de Bonneville, a former professor of French at Harvard College. De Bonneville had been traveling around the country advocating *mesmerism* (also known as "animal magnetism"), a therapeutic practice based on the notion that magnetic forces could be transmitted to relieve pain. During this period, magnetism had become a focus of mind-body debate. Among the believers was Harriet Martineau, who published on the topic and practiced it on others. Despite the fact that mesmerism had not gained respect in the medical community, Edmund saw potential in its effects on the human nervous system. He claimed that de Bonneville had stopped his chill within two minutes. After that experience, Edmund gave much thought to animal magnetism as a possible cure for his deafness as well. "Many things he does are to me incomprehensible as I cannot hear his lecture yet and can get no books on the subject," he wrote to Mary Ann on January 18, 1844. "Some laugh at me and some say I cannot be cured."[8]

Despite his health problems, Edmund accompanied Clark Walworth to Iowa City with a load of flour. There were several inches of snow on the ground, so he dressed himself in his drawers, two pair of pantaloons, two vests, a coat, and a larger overcoat. He also wore two pair of thick stockings and tied a heavy bed quilt around his neck, which he slung over his head.

At the time, Mary Ann's brother George was a member of the Territorial Legislature at Iowa City. Edmund visited with George for several days and was about to leave the city when the assistant clerk of the House of Representatives, in need of a clerk, suggested that the deaf man remain for a while to help. Edmund agreed to begin on February 5, 1844. During his stay in Iowa City, Edmund wrote a series of letters to Mary Ann in which he further described his experiments with animal magnetism. George had no faith in such cures, but Edmund bet him ten hogs that the treatment would improve his hearing. "I may be disappointed but I have very strong confidence," Edmund said.[9]

Edmund had learned about a young girl in Hartford who had been magnetized at the American Asylum. He knew that Mary Ann's parents also had no faith in animal magnetism. While he believed that de Bonneville was legitimate, he did warn her family about quacks.

[L]et me entreat you never on any account to allow Mary Ann to be magnetized in any way whatever by persons calling themselves professors of the science or who have seen others do it. Magnetism (or Mesmerism) is, like

Edmund Booth (above) and Mary Ann Walworth Booth (next page) in the 1850s. From the Booth family album, courtesy of The Haggin Museum, Stockton, California.

fire, "a good friend but a dangerous enemy." In the hands of ignorance or presumption it will throw a person into convulsive fits, hard and long to cure, or render him idiotic for life. Mary Ann, you must be cautious.[10]

At this time in his life, Edmund began to grow disenchanted with living on the prairie. He appeared to miss the intellectual challenges of teaching, yet he showed no indication that he desired to return to that profession. Rather, he seemed to be considering his options for a nonfarming occupation where he could use his mind more than his hands. He wrote to Mary Ann that the idea of returning home to Buffalo Forks would be "sheer

nonsense. You know it is a stupid place except enlivened by folly; and that three fourths of the inhabitants are blockheads or knaves. All the children that can, will be off; and once off, they will never come back if they can help it." He was also frustrated over recent financial troubles; he needed to earn enough money to visit her and Thomas "before going to that paradise of all dullness the Buffalo [Forks]."[11]

In this letter of January 18, Edmund also inquired about his son: "How does he grow—talk—play—do mischief, etc? I hope we shall bring him up properly that he may be something better than a man who merely vegetated and died."[12] With mesmerism occupying his thoughts, he seemed conflicted about Mary Ann leaving her family, wanting her to stay until they investigated whether her deafness could be cured. He had gone to Bloomington in search of de Bonneville, but the mesmerist had left that town. On February 6, he wrote a letter by a good fire, although the room was so cold he had to stop and thaw his fingers every few minutes. Suffering with earaches, he remained hopeful that the magnetism he had received would work.

> De B—told me to stay in the house when weather is cold. The clairvoyant says I shall certainly hear as soon as warm weather comes and De B—tells me to have patience till then. When I go to Burlington he will get the wax out of the ear, first putting me into sound magnetic sleep. He will not use any instrument of the Doctors, but will draw it out by magnetism.[13]

Edmund had seen De Bonneville demonstrate his techniques on about twenty different people in Bloomington. In his February letters, he harbored increasing hope that Mary Ann's deafness might be cured if her eardrums and nerves were not damaged. "I intend he shall examine you and if he says you can be cured you shall be if it can be done before he leaves St. Louis. As soon as it is known at Greenville that he is in St. Louis Father must take you there and call on him and be examined."[14]

Through February, the soreness in his own ears plagued him and he apparently experienced tinnitus. He told Mary Ann that "when they ache I ask Geo. to magnetize them and he gets out all the pain in a few seconds. They itch very much and the drums of the ears ring softly at night. At

Dubuque after being magnetized and before the oils were put in, they rang very often every day as if I had a pistol fired within them. I do not yet understand magnetism well."[15]

Little is known about Edmund's financial problems at this time. The only mention appears in a letter he wrote to Mary Ann—"the winter has in general been rather mild. Since I last wrote you I have rec'd. a letter from Mr. Bigelow in which was enclosed my final discharge in bankruptcy so I am once more a free man. So give three cheers for my sake and I will try and paddle my canoe a little more cautiously in future." In this same letter, he expressed his desire to see her: "I hope you are making up your mind to come up in the Spring as I am fully satisfied that it will contribute to the general [happiness] of us all to be together."[16] Within a week, he received a letter from Mary Ann dated January 31, which included a note from her mother as well. He responded to Mary Ann on February 13, saying, "I felt much affected on reading your and Mother's remarks about yourself and Thomas." At the same time, he seemed worried that Mary Ann's parents were considering moving back to Iowa. Edmund was not happy living there himself, so he added a note to his in-laws: "Father and mother. . . . If you remove there [Iowa] you will expect Mary Ann to remain near you and she will feel a separation too hard and will of course wish to stay in a place which we both heartily detest."[17] Edmund had talked to Clark and George about an alternative plan to have their parents move to a new location that would allow them to see their family more often by traveling on the Mississippi. Although most of Mary Ann's correspondence during her stay in Round Prairie, Illinois, was lost, later letters reveal tension between Edmund and her parents in 1844.[18]

In this same letter, Edmund again expressed hope that one day Mary Ann would learn to speak, possibly through animal magnetism: "I have better hopes now for both you and me than ever before. A disappointment will not hurt us much because we are used to the rack, but I am very sure that De B—will cure wherever he says he will. . . . I suppose I shall have the pleasure of teaching you to *speak*. . . . if a cure is pronounced possible I will have it done if it costs all our property."[19]

He also gave advice to Mary Ann about raising their son.

Tell Thomas Papa will see him in the spring. From your and mother's account he improves faster than I well dared expect. I knew he would rise above common (from his head and size of lungs) but I feared at times that it might be a father's partiality. Of all things in children I hate excess vanity—Do not cause his to grow more than possible. It is large enough already and I fear too large. . . . I wish you would cultivate in Thomas as much as possible the feeling of *conscience* by gentle means so that his honesty may not spring from *fear*.[20]

❧❦❧

EDMUND continued working for the Iowa Legislature through February 1844. It is uncertain how he kept up with the rapid-fire communication in the House meetings. Throughout his life, he never complained about the isolation resulting from deafness or the communication barriers he experienced. He just found ways to go over, under, and around these barriers and live his life to the fullest. In Iowa City he managed somehow to pick up the legislative details, including the scheduling of an extra session in June for Iowa to take steps for entering the Union of the States. He most likely learned this from his brother-in-law George, who would be attending that session. Edmund also shared a room with a member of the council and one of the editors of a newspaper, and the editor may have shared some of his notes with him. Relying on his one healthy eye, he recorded many of his own observations as well. During one session, Governor John Chambers entered the House arm-in-arm with the chief of a band of Sacs and Foxes that was living near Iowa City. Chambers, who had served in the War of 1812, had been governor since 1841, after serving in the Kentucky legislature for some years. The accompanying chief's hauteur, with his full Indian costume and repeated rearrangement of the dense row of plumage in his headdress, left Edmund and the entire House curious. Soon after, a score of Indians in full regalia entered the room, creating a stir; the speaker desperately rapped to order, and the entire House assumed a professional decorum. Edmund, unable to hear the debate, nevertheless capably summarized a critical issue addressed in this session—women's suffrage.

That question had begun to be agitated and the agitation had extended to Iowa. Petitions to allow women to vote were in vogue and an afternoon was set for discussing the matter. The house assembled and a good number of ladies of Iowa City took seats among the members, there being a small lobby but no gallery. I could not but notice that the aspect of the ladies was different from their every-day appearance in that body. They seemed to belong to the thoughtful class. There was nothing of the gay or frivolous or desire of show in their dress or looks. They sat silent, eyes downcast for the most part, lips almost compressed as if resolved to endure under wrong, and yet possessed of resolution to have the wrong righted in the end, however distant that end might be. . . . Doubtless there were those who felt that it was a large subject, too large for the time to settle or dispose of, but two or three went into regular spread-eagleism and aired their shallowness, their conceit and their devotion to women, as a parlor ornament.[21]

Edmund's stance on women's suffrage was indicative of things to come. He developed an egalitarian perspective that would surface in many forms throughout his life and help define him as a great man.

After the legislative session closed, Edmund left Iowa City to visit Mary Ann in Bond County. He first traveled to Burlington in a two-horse buggy. The secretary of the House, whose last name was Burr, and another man were with him. It was now March and the roads were in good shape. It took two days to travel about 80 miles through continuous prairie. Occasionally they saw groves of oak trees, but no more than a half dozen dwellings made of logs during the whole trip. The first night they stayed with a family in one of the log houses. At Wapello, they met Senator Springer, whose office was a frame shanty a little larger than a hen coop. Edmund marveled at finding the lawyer in, "as it then appeared, so uncompromising a spot."[22]

At the Mississippi, they had to cross an ice bridge. Each man held a stout pole about ten-to fifteen feet long. "Not a house nor a mortal was in sight, and should the ice give way—what?" This nearly happened, as Edmund later described:

Burr took the lead, stepped carefully forward and proceeded along with the same care. I followed a rod behind, and the slim man brought up the rear at an equal distance. We were midway across, stepping quickly and lightly, Indian fashion, each holding his pole horizontally as a support in case of a plunge. Suddenly my boot heel went through; I drew it out and kept on, for it was no time to dally, but the slim man stopped in affright and spoke. Burr stopped, turned with anxiety on his face and an almost angry shake of his head; I glanced back, saw the look of terror on the slim man's countenance and the exact impress of my boot heel through the thin ice; looked again at Burr, and here we were, all three standing stock still. The whole thing, for the moment, was excessively comical, and in spite of the danger I exploded. Burr looked around thoughtfully and changed his course. I followed as before, and the slim man made a *detour* to avoid tumbling into the boot heel hole behind me. Finally we reached the bank safe.[23]

Edmund finally arrived in Round Prairie in April. Though he was glad to be with Mary Ann and Thomas, he found the Walworth home life extremely dull. They had no books, and reading meant much to him. He devoured every book and newspaper he could find. He also had some disagreements with his in-laws during this visit. After three months helping the family on the farm, "rather existing than living," Edmund noted sarcastically, he returned to Iowa, leaving Mary Ann and Thomas to come later. Mary Ann wished to stay for a while longer to help her mother with spinning and weaving. This plan failed, however, for everyone except Thomas became sick.

Edmund's trip home in June was uneventful. Back home, the monotony of farming quickly took its toll on the educated deaf man's patience. He had written to Mary Ann in February that he was ready "to sell all and abandon the county for I am heartily sick of it." [24] That sentiment now worsened. He found relief with the weekly *New York Tribune,* to which he subscribed. Once a week he walked nearly 20 miles round-trip to get his mail. He was becoming restless. To make matters worse, the mail was so slow that letters sat in the post office for three weeks or more before they were picked up. August came with Mary Ann still in Illinois; Edmund had not gotten any mail from her. He wrote to her that he was expecting her in September, since her father had promised to bring her home. However, she did not return until much later in the fall.[25]

In February 1845, Mary Ann received a touching letter from her mother, in which Philura compared the love Mary Ann had shown for young Thomas to her own love for Mary Ann, particularly after she had become deaf:

What were our fond hopes, how pleasing our prospects. But I know your sufferings, your privations. Here I stop: it is too painful for me to dwell upon. I will only say to you, my dear child, if you are ever made to doubt the sincerity of your parents love to you, think how much you love your child. . . . If you had as many sons and daughters as we have had, you would have the same love for them all, and it would make you very happy to see them kind and affectionate to each other. It has been my happiness too. . . . I hope you still retain natural affection for your parents, brothers and sisters, who feel so much for you.[26]

Over the next year, the Booths farmed their land as they had done in the past. On February 22, 1846, Mary Ann gave birth to a daughter. Edmund prepared for the birth of their second child by moving the family to more comfortable quarters.

Before another winter came, the first winter on the open prairie just south of Dutch or Reed's Creek having proved too uncomfortable, I pulled down the log cabin and hauled the logs to the newly laid out town of Fairview, nearly one mile north within the borders of the timber, having purchased the lot of Clement Russell and in a few hours the logs were put in place and the roof of split, unshaven shingles laid on the roof pole, fastened by other poles and no nails, as was the custom of the time. We moved in and enjoyed life about as much as is given to mortals to enjoy. In this house a girl was born, named Harriet.[27]

Farming life was all-consuming and often dangerous. Prairie fires burned for miles, forcing farmers to fight to save their grain and hay stacks. Even in the settled areas there were dangers. One day, while visiting the Walworth Mills with his mother, young Thomas was trampled by several horses. His uncle Denison rescued him but not in time to avoid a hoof in the face that left a scar across the bridge of his nose. That scar served as a lifelong reminder to Thomas of how close he had come to being killed.

Mary Ann was fortunate to have spent the time with her parents in Bond County in 1844. George and Philura Walworth did move to Iowa in 1846, but Philura died on September 27 of that year, and George died on March 21, 1847. The deaf couple would experience still more tragedy within a short time. A few months after George's death, Harriet died at the age of seventeen months.[28] This was indeed a tragic blow to Mary Ann, who desperately wanted to raise a large family. To their great happiness, a second daughter was born in that same log house on June 17, 1848. She was also named Harriet and nicknamed Hattie.

That summer, Edmund grew 15 acres of crops, but there was not much of a market. He and Henry took hogs and wheat to Dubuque, where they were able to do better business. Still, the Booths lived in relatively primitive conditions. Edmund took advantage of every opportunity to improve their lives, as the following story demonstrates:

> Henry and I had no wagon and no money to buy one. Could be obtained only in Dubuque, price $80 or more, and I concluded to put my knowledge of carpenter's tools to use. Found a log by the roadside, 20 inches diameter, that had been cut and removed out of the way by the men who had laid out the Military road. . . . Borrowed a cross-cut saw, two inch auger, and $1^{1}/_{2}$ inch chisel of Clement Russell. Sawed four wheels from the log, each about five or six inches wide. Bored a hole through each and, with the chisel, cut out the center four inches diameter. Made axle trees . . . fixed a reach that would work easy and allow turning around, and with stakes at all the corners, had a very convenient wagon for logs, wood and so forth.[29]

By this time Edmund had, beside the oxen, a cow or two, calves, and a dozen or more hogs. His white-faced cow had a fierce temper and was dangerous when anyone approached her new calf. One afternoon, the cow and calf escaped to a grove some distance from the house. Edmund decided to drive them home. Thomas, who followed his father in search of the animals, summarized the adventure as follows:

> The calf was found under a small tree. So father picked up the calf, which of course commenced a frantic bleating. Almost instantly the cow plunged in through the thicket, struck father in the breast with her horns and thrust him against the tall, heavy hazel brush. I jumped behind the tree and fortunately the cow didn't notice me. Father was a giant in strength, seized the horns of the cow and turned her aside, with no serious results to himself, though I remember most vividly how he was borne downward in the hazel brush and how frightened I was.[30]

To give some balance to the monotony of farming life, Edmund sought community involvement. He was an especially strong advocate for the education of deaf children. After Iowa became a state (December 28, 1846), Edmund encouraged the Iowa legislature to support sending deaf children to the Illinois institution in Jacksonville and to financially provide for their education. The legislature agreed to pay half of the children's expenses; the parents paid the other half. The first students from Iowa included Dennis A. Dewey from Iowa City, and Mary Ann True from Greensburg; they entered the Illinois school in 1848.

⁂

IN 1848, Edmund learned that John Sutter, a Swiss immigrant, and James Marshall had stumbled upon gold nuggets near a sawmill on the American River at Coloma, California. Reports of gold discoveries soon followed from areas of the Feather River and Trinity River. These stories were validated by President James Polk. Edmund's interest increased further with the writings of Horace Greeley in the *New York Tribune*. He followed the excitement in the newspapers for months and watched as teams of wagons, filled with "emigrants," passed by daily on the military road near his home.

"Gold fever" struck Edmund Booth early in the spring of 1849—"I began to feel like falling in with the throng. I had grown a little tired of the round of farm life and small profits."[31] He believed that he, too, could find gold, and so he began making plans to go to California.

FOUR

On the California Trail

❧❧❧

LIKE thousands of young men who never dreamed that they would leave their families, Edmund Booth hoped that joining the California Gold Rush would help him provide for Mary Ann and his children in a much better way than farming on the Iowa frontier. The adventurer in him was a driving force in his decision to leave his family. He was 38 years old and he chafed at the limitations of life on the prairie. With Hattie and Thomas to raise, Mary Ann agreed to move in with Edmund's brother Henry, Henry's daughter, and Edmund's mother, Martha Eyre Booth. Like Edmund, Henry had a passion for reading, and at the end of a day's labor he would read aloud to his aged mother from the works of Walter Scott and other authors. Edmund thought this might be a good environment for his children while he was gone to the gold mines.

Lewis Perkins helped Edmund rebuild a covered wagon for the trip West. The wagon bed was new and was divided into compartments for salt, pork, hams, potatoes, hard crackers, and other food, as well as bedding necessities. Using Henry's box stove with tin side ovens shaped like two halves of a barrel split lengthwise, Mary Ann spent her days baking crackers and filling the wagon with them.

Benjamin Clough, another former pupil of the Hartford school, was living in Anamosa at this time and he decided to join Edmund on the journey to California. Clough was about two years older than Edmund. He had been deafened by "spotted fever" at the age of six, and had entered the American Asylum in 1825 at the age of seventeen. He stayed only two years. Clough lost his father, a farmer, when he was a young boy. Sent to get his father's horse, he and his two brothers sensed danger and feared that the horse would kick them. Their father came to help and the boys saw their father thrown from the horse and die. Like Edmund, Clough had to accept additional responsibilities for his family. Such a lesson in life likely helped both men develop the survival skills they required for the long trek to California.[1]

As the Booth family helped Edmund prepare for the overland journey, Thomas offered to mold bullets for his father's gun by melting the balls in his mother's pewter syrup cup. Mary Ann would not permit this for practical as well as sentimental reasons. Edmund's mother was also averse to firearms, fearing Edmund would lose his remaining eye.

On May 9, 1849, Edmund and Clough set out for the land of gold in a covered wagon pulled by several yokes of oxen. Edmund also took Towser, the family dog. They had delayed the start of their journey until there was enough green grass for feeding the oxen along the way. Henry Booth went with them to make sure everything started off right, and then he returned to Anamosa. Nearly a week later, on Tuesday, May 15, Edmund wrote his first letter to Mary Ann.

> We are now camped on the prairies with our faces westward. The sun an hour high and shining into the wagon on me as I am writing. . . . behind is a brook and three teams for California from Bellevue, Jackson Co. owned by young men with their wives just married—fine looking young men. We are (in our company) four teams—one of them we met at the Cedar River and [that] was the one that passed through Fairview two or three days before I started, and has two cows. They are now churning for butter and do that every night. . . . we have as much buttermilk as we wish; and every morning we have milk for our coffee; and have had butter daily. . . . This team is owned by a Mr. Wm. Smith (an old man of somewhere about 70 but hearty and joyous as a boy) and his son-in-law and family.[2]

Edmund never explained how he acquired the many details he shared in his letters during his long journey on the California Trail. He learned people's names, information about the places he passed along the trail, and facts about weather, troubles with Indians, and other tidbits that other emigrants usually learned in the course of conversation with each other.

He apparently was a very amicable man, aggressive about his communication needs, but in a way that won over the admiration of others and encouraged them to make the extra effort necessary to communicate with a profoundly deaf person. Edmund did not have much confidence in his ability to read lips, so he used gestures and carried a notebook and pencil with him. Perhaps he taught the manual alphabet (fingerspelling) and a few basic signs to some of the emigrants. Such would certainly have provided a bit of relief to the monotony of wagon travel, which averaged only 10 to 20 miles per day. In his May 15 letter, he wrote to Mary Ann,

> We are now near sixty miles from home, and have been on the road a week. Today we traveled about fifteen miles. You will be surprised to know that we have traveled so short a distance in so long a time. The reason is bad roads, bad weather, and desire that the cattle feed well now that the grass has just become plenty enough. As the distance is so short, I will give some description of the journey, for it will be impossible for me to do so in detail in future letters. We left, I believe on Wednesday.
>
> . . . Had such a thing happened today [the wagon bogging down in the mud] I should have got out without difficulty and without unloading but the cattle were not then used to the work. As it was, we could not release the wagon, though we unloaded it. We let the animals feed for about three hours when I took them to "Gilbert's" and chained them for the night, I lodging at that place, while Clough remained in the wagon. I returned in the morning, and in two hours the Dubuque teams arrived and put on their cattle and drew the wagon out of the mud.[3]

After arriving at the Cedar River and camping, the wagon train began to cross over, but the rain delayed them for another day. The travelers camped south of the Cedar, on an island with running water nearby. They left the Cedar River on Saturday morning and traveled about 5 miles when it began to rain again. They stopped at a good camping place, and, seeing no prospect of abatement, Edmund unyoked his oxen. When his company arrived at Iowa City, they obtained supplies and then crossed the Iowa River and camped. The next morning, they traveled a mile or so and came on a very steep hill that seemed "almost perpendicular" to Edmund. A good stout rope was attached to the rear axle of each wagon with both hind wheels locked and with all but the wheel cattle taken off, the rope was passed once around a tree at the top of the hill and with men holding on to it, the wagons were let down the hill.

Shortly after that, they encountered still another problem resulting from the rain. The bridge across Clear Creek had been carried off and lay high and dry on the shore. The water was about eight-feet deep, so Edmund's company made a float of four logs and a few planks from the bridge. By means of a rope held by men on each side, they ferried their baggage, provisions, and, finally, the empty wagons. They then reloaded their wagons, transported the animals over the creek, and set up camp.

The next morning Edmund yoked his wild ox without any difficulty. "Good treatment has cured him of his wildness," he wrote to Mary Ann. "They would never have been wild if they had not had wild masters." The steer only required watching and directing when the wagons were taken off the road to avoid deep ruts. The group was now 250 miles from Council Bluffs, which they expected to reach in 25 days. Edmund told Mary Ann that he would write to her from there or from Trader's Point, Iowa, opposite Council Bluffs. "We calculate to reach the gold country (California) about the first of Oct.," he wrote, but "I think we shall not till the middle or later. We shall go over the Sierra Nevada anyhow. We can break a road; and a thousand Yankees like those I see on the way are not to be stopped by a few feet of snow or a 9,000 foot mountain."[4]

Edmund's company made him feel as if they had all lived together for twenty years. "I have not yet begun to feel dull or discouraged. The fact is, the fatigue and difficulties of the journey are more in the imagination than in reality."[5] He was excited about crossing the American continent— the Indian country, the Great Basin, South Pass, the Sierra Nevada—and setting foot on the shores of the Pacific. His May 15 letter to Mary Ann was typical of those he would write in terms of the great detail he provided about his daily activities.

> Our wagon is our house and stored with provisions and that is the utmost that many of our neighbors have. Few of them care for aught save a house and enough to eat. At the City I obtained the Republican (newspaper) of

> May 9. . . . I had no time when at the City to write you as I was busy every
> moment, the men not desiring to wait longer than necessary for me, having
> completed their own outfit at Dubuque. . . . We find our bed very comfort-
> able and sleep soundly.[6]

Edmund soon learned that a double cover was necessary at the top of
the wagon hoops to keep out the rain. On Wednesday, May 16, the wagons traveled 18 miles, 15 more on Thursday. The roads were drying rapidly, which helped the company travel faster, sometimes 20 miles a day.
Edmund saw only one house during these two days.

> We are getting along well. Have not yet broken anything and have proved
> the strength of the wagon with nine yoke of oxen. The Bellevue people keep
> near us behind and a few miles back we see three more teams—do not know
> where from. I hope you are well and doing well. I will have a letter ready
> for you by the time we reach the Bluffs. Write me there.[7]

The roads they took next at first appeared to become better as they
traveled westward. In one day they crossed more than a dozen bridges.
The worst road Edmund encountered was one between Fairview and the
Cedar River. He was very optimistic during this early stage of the journey
and felt fortunate to have Clough with him. His deaf companion not only
conversed in sign language with him but was a first-rate cook. "You know I
never was good as a cook," he wrote to Mary Ann. In this letter, Edmund
reminded her that he enjoyed this sort of life. He also explained that he
was pleased with the family dog. "Tell Thomas that Towser has plenty to
eat among the wagons, is well liked and proves a good watch dog. Will fly
at every man that comes from the other company of wagons or from the
neighborhood."[8]

When he arrived at Council Bluffs, he looked for a post office. But
expecting to receive a letter from Mary Ann was too hopeful. The mail
delivery in both directions was very unreliable. On May 21, he posted his
first letter, "or rather journal for it has assumed that form. . . . I have thus
given you something of a journal and you see our mode of life."[9] He
mailed it from a post office he found 95 miles west of Iowa City. His

company encountered two bad holes to cross and two bridges. They traveled over the north fork of the Skunk River on a bridge about 60-feet long and so narrow that there was no room for the driver. Edmund crossed with his cattle, walking on the guards all the way, which were made from small trees. That night they camped in a wooded area in a heavy rain. A team of wagons soon came up that Edmund had seen in Anamosa ten days before he started. It was from Dubuque and had been detained by bad roads. That team decided to join them, making eight teams in the company, all from Iowa. They numbered eighteen men, four women, two small children, and over eighty head of cattle, including four cows.

Within two weeks, Edmund's company had increased to about sixty people, but by the time they reached the troublesome Loup Fork of the Platte River (in what is now Nebraska), three men had died of cholera. The cause was probably bacteria in the drinking water and the food. Edmund and his fellow emigrants were in the wilderness, and without means of communication, they did not know the extent of the cholera outbreak in the country.

Edmund himself nearly died at the Loup Fork. On a warm June night when he was standing guard from midnight until daylight, he began to feel cold. Suspecting that he had cholera, he sought warmth from a cooking fire. As the cold feeling increased, he went to his wagon and took a half dozen mandrake pills, thinking that he might as well die of an overdose as of cholera. The pills, made from the mandrake plant, were often used for headache, constipation, indigestion, and liver and kidney illness. They were thought to purify the blood.

Worried that his own death was imminent, Edmund thought of his family back home. When daylight arrived, he took over twenty mandrake pills, entered the wagon, and covered himself with blankets. After feeling no warmth, he woke up his partner and asked him to go to Captain Compton to borrow a couple of buffalo robes. Compton came afterwards and looked gravely at him, offering Edmund a bottle of painkiller medicine.

I took a swallow from the bottle and felt no smart or heat in the liquid. Took another and another, and drank it all and no taste, smart or heat.

Returned Compton the empty bottle and lay down. From his looks I
thought he judged I was done for. In a half hour or less felt like vomiting.
Called for the wash basin and vomited plenty of *cold* water. In so doing
began to grow warm and perspire and then knew I was safe. . . . It needed
heroic treatment and had it. I was the fourth of the company taken with the
cholera and the only one that lived.[10]

The brawny deaf man recovered rather quickly from his bout with the
disease. The following morning he had a breakfast of fried ham, beans,
crackers, salt pork, and coffee.

Along with the cholera, the rough terrain, and the weather conditions,
the company also encountered some trouble with Pawnee Indians. Near
the Loup Fork, Edmund's wagon train was stopped by a dozen Indians
armed and standing across the road. They demanded $10 for allowing the
wagons to cross their land. Edmund saw some 200 other Indian men,
women, and children moving about on the hills nearly a mile away.
Among those traveling with Edmund was Colonel William Hamilton, the
son of Alexander Hamilton, President Washington's Secretary of the Trea-
sury who was killed in a duel with Aaron Burr. Col. Hamilton had attended West Point, and he took charge of the company. He ordered the
men to prepare their arms and then gave the order to move forward. Fortunately, the Indians moved and stood by the road as Edmund and his
fellow emigrants passed. There was no further trouble and Edmund wondered if the Indians possibly feared the cholera more than the guns.

It was now nearly a month since Edmund had left Fairview. Day after
day they proceeded up the left side of the Platte River, the road nearly
level all the way. On one occasion, a wagon axle broke, so the company
stopped while a few men took an axe, crossed the Platte, cut down a tree,
and brought back the trunk for the blacksmith to make a new axle. Edmund worried that his letters were not reaching Mary Ann. He saw others
writing, and they appeared to have more confidence in the mail. Since he
had left in early May, he had mailed letters to her from Newton, Jasper
County, and Fort Des Moines. "I am not very sanguine," he told her on
June 5, "you will even receive this. Nevertheless I will write."[11]

The journey was fairly uneventful over the next 500 miles on the

California Trail. Edmund saw only one small herd of buffalo. Several of the men took off after the buffalo and brought meat back for the group. Edmund enjoyed "the first fresh meat [he] had seen since leaving civilization." The next stop was Fort Laramie, Wyoming, "a board stockade with sentry boxes on the corners, a broad gateway for teams, and a large dwelling house inside for men and officers."[12] The fort was a common stop for wagon trains, where travelers rested and purchased new supplies before crossing the Rocky Mountains. Edmund's group stayed only one night before continuing on their way. To prepare for the trip, Edmund had read John C. Fremont's book, *Report of the Exploring Expedition to the Rocky Mountains.* He brought the book with him, and he knew what to expect along the way.[13] The other men in his company were not as well informed.

On August 1, the wagons reached the South Pass, the gate of the Rocky Mountains. It had been three months since they left Iowa. "It is the same barren desert we had been traveling for nearly a month—no grass—nothing but sand, pebbles and wild sage."[14] As one reads Edmund's daily entries in full, it becomes evident that his journal was a sanctuary, perhaps like a confidante with whom to talk and shape his being. In doing this he never feared being bored as he captured his routine in detail. While reading the long descriptions one can imagine sitting next to him on his wagon and seeing the world as he did. Although blind in one eye, he missed little as he emptied his mind onto the pages of this journal.

For her part, Mary Ann could do nothing but wait until Edmund reached Sacramento to tell him about her own travails over the five months he traveled on the California Trail. While slightly less adventurous than her husband's overland journey, the deaf woman's life in Iowa was arduous. Over the subsequent years that Edmund spent in California, Mary Ann took on more responsibility and experienced more deprivation than most hearing women of her time. As a deaf woman who did not use her speech, she also faced the frustrating challenges of communicating with townsfolk and strangers alike.

THE days went by slowly in August. Edmund continued to regularly record his observations of the weather, grass conditions for feeding the animals, and distance traveled per day. Each night he and his companions spread their beds on the ground with the sky for their canopy. Sometimes the rain was light, but enough to break up sleep. Early in the month, they

> stopped along the road sides—made fires of wild sage and boiled our coffee. Nothing but a sandy desert everywhere, covered with bunches of short, stunted wild sage. We straggled down to the ford of the Green River in a most pitiable plight. Cattle feeble from starvation, thirst and 20 hours hard drawing. All sleepy and weary. The last night was rather coldish, and the men in advance kindled fires by the road with wild sage—as they went along.[15]

On Sunday, August 6, the thirty-team train found a tributary stream of Green River with a good supply of grass. The next day Edmund's company remained in camp to allow the animals to rest again. The wild ox and red steer were giving out and would die if starved much longer. Recent rain had wet the surface of the parched earth and five camps along the stream gave the place a lively appearance. The name of the stream, an old trader told him, was Fontanelle, named for Logan Fontanelle, a chief of the Omaha tribe. The trader had been to California and appeared familiar with the route. He told Edmund that the distance from their camp to Sutter's Mill was 727 miles and that they must go by Fort Hall.

On Tuesday, August 8, the wagon train started at noon and traveled about 12 miles before making camp on the Thomas Fork of the Bear River, northeast of the Great Salt Lake. They found plenty of fish and wild ducks and rejoiced at their "good fortune in coming safely this route, saving at least ten days."[16] The land was very broken, with an abundance of fir, cottonwood, and willow groves. They came to a small rushing stream running south where the Washington City Company had watered. By August 11, they arrived at Bear River and camped near a grove of willows near six or seven other camps. Half of the teams left within a short time. It was a fine morning and Edmund noted in his journal the beautiful wide valley. A slow stream ran north, and as they broke up camp on the morning of August 12, Edmund saw clouds of dust among the hills on the right, indicating the arrival of emigrants they had left at Fontanelle. They were now over 5,000 feet above sea level and could feel the sun's warmth.

Edmund's group made slow, but steady, progress over the next two weeks. On Friday, August 24, 1849, sitting by the Raft River where they had stopped, Edmund recorded a special note in his journal.

> Tried roasted and fried [mussels]. Some liked them. Some did not. At 1/2 hour before sunset, camped on a small stream running south. Think we have crossed into the Great Basin again. Clough's wild ox lay down on the road and he was compelled to fall behind till it had fed. I was a mile ahead of the train. On learning the fact, I went back to help him. Found him coming on. He takes it in good part. Says he will pack on his back or on the other ox as long as it holds out. We push on too fast for our animals. Have thus far beaten all ox teams we have come in sight of, and are ahead of all the mule trains except that of St. Louis. This day I am 39 years.[17]

With little grass available, two members of Edmund's team (Compton and Every) both lost oxen. The company traveled 7 miles to Goose Creek, a branch of Lewis Fork of the Columbia River, and camped there to rest the cattle. One of the boys traveling with them shot a wild duck, which they ate with bean soup for supper. They were now about 100 miles from the Humboldt River. Their eleven wagons arrived at Hot Spring in Spring Valley, and after traveling 15 more miles they rested for two hours at noon. Grass was abundant in the valley as were the willows, which the emigrants cut down for firewood. On September 5, the company passed twelve Mormon teams returning to Salt Lake from California. The Mormons had left the Bay of San Francisco on July 16. They told Edmund that there was plenty of gold in California.[18]

For the next five days Edmund's company crossed hills and mountains as they traveled southwest into Utah territory. On September 10, they made camp near the south end of the Salt Lake. Dusty and fatigued, they boiled coffee and ate bread for supper before they slept. Edmund had been on the trail for four months. "We are now about 190 miles from . . . the river," he wrote, "and are getting impatient for the end of the journey."[19]

As the wagon train progressed along the California Trail, Edmund saw written notices warning emigrants to look out for their animals, which were being stolen at night. "We drove in ours last night and shall attend to them nightly for the remainder of the journey on this road." Despite the efforts to guard the cattle, one member of the company, named Knudsen, had all his cattle stolen. "Some of our men went with him to hunt his animals," Edmund wrote in his journal. "Meanwhile we . . . went on, taking his wagon with us to the next camping."[20]

Knudsen returned the favor the following week when a storm struck. "By good fortune Knudsen has a tent and thus I escaped a drenching." Three of the wagon trains, Missouri, Arkansas, and Independent, with over twenty wagons, were now traveling as one, and "almost every train [had] fewer wagons than when east of the South Pass."[21]

The company continued on through Nevada. They crossed three rivers but could not find sufficient grass for the cattle. On Sunday, September 23, four Indians came into the camp while the company was having breakfast.

> We, as usual, gave them bread, meat and coffee. One of them undertook to guide us to grass. In a half hour we came to a good running stream 2 or 3 yards wide with abundance of tall fine grass—the best I have seen on the river yet. Here we found a camp of six wagons and the famous Indian chief Truckee. He understands English enough to be understood and . . . gave directions for the route to the Truckee river. Some 20 of his tribe are among us and are the most civilized Indians I ever met. It is evident they are familiar with the whites. Saw lumps of gold among them. Cut hay and remained in camp all day to prepare the animals for the journey to the . . . (Truckee) river.[22]

Edmund's group broke camp the next morning and traveled until late in the evening with the hope of finding good drinking water.

> We drove a mile this morning and found several wells. One contained tolerable water which we gave our animals and used ourselves. Filled our jugs, and, half a mile further, we came to the stream. . . . It was a mere slough of very bad water and near it under a bluff was a well of good water of which

we made use. Drove on all day in the desert. Course west of south. It was evident we were on the wrong road going to Carson River. Found wells, some of alkali and some of salt. Gave our animals some of the former. Drove till near 12 at night, hoping to find better water. My red ox gave out before this time. We now came to two wagons which had sent on their teams 11 miles to the river to recruit. After a mile further, Compton returned from exploring. We tied up our animals without feed or water, our hay being gone. We were now ten miles from the river. It was a desperate day's journey.[23]

The next day they started before daybreak without breakfast. They lost two more head of cattle and knew they must reach water before noon or half of their animals would die. The alkali and saltwater made both humans and animals very thirsty. After 4 miles, one of Edmund's companions, Oscar, came in from the river. He had gone ahead the day before and now carried an India-rubber canteen of good water. Soon after this, one of Edmund's oxen gave out, but without lying down. "I unyoked, but could not make him advance one step. I left him on the road."[24] Edmund saw other oxen, one after another, give out and lie down every few minutes but he would not give up on his own ox. He walked 3 miles down the road with it and carried three pails of water, a bundle of hay, and a large bunch of willows to the animal.

In the evening I got him in, with much trouble from his obstinacy, until when within 1/4 mile of the river he smelled water and came with a quick pace. The quantity he drank caused me some uneasiness. He went across and in 1/2 hour another was brought in a worse condition and drank in the same way. . . . Thus we are through the desert, having traveled over 50 miles—the men say 60—and the most dangerous part of the journey. Much of the desert is encrusted with salt and alkali. Mirage is common and the illusion complete. All day men have passed up and down the road carrying water to such animals as have given out and to sick men, left to guard the wagons behind.[25]

After another moonless night, Edmund went looking for his red steer. He saw over 100 loose mules and two mule wagons and, a few miles farther, came upon the "Pioneer Line" of passenger wagons. He finally found his steer tied to a wagon 11 miles from his camp. Edmund drove the steer 3 miles until the animal lay down and would not rise. Edmund left him there and returned to camp. "The road up and across the desert is strewed with carcasses of oxen, horses, mules and abandoned wagons almost numberless," he wrote, knowing that soon his steer would be among them.[26]

Edmund's company left this western region of what is now Nevada at noon on September 28, with only three wagons. Edmund had given up his own wagon and put his remaining team on one of the others. The group traveled 20 miles on a stony road along the Carson River. The next day they moved only 3 miles before setting up camp. They knew that 9 miles of very heavy sand lay ahead of them, so they decided to traverse that distance in the cool of the evening. They crossed the Carson River on October 1 and traveled on its right bank until sunset. They were in a gorge, surrounded on all sides by mountains. "This morning the atmosphere was clear of haze and we saw the snowy peaks of the Sierra Nevada before us. . . . Nights growing cold and shows we are ascending to higher regions."[27]

Over the next few days Edmund recorded seeing smoke from Indian campfires on the Sierra Nevada Mountains. The route was rough, stony, and uphill. He saw more warnings on the roadside about stolen cattle. Edmund and his companions tried to get their equipment and tired stock up the canyon but only made it 3 miles. The Pioneer Line's passenger and baggage wagons were also having difficulty getting around the rocks and they plugged the trail for a day. Edmund's group unhooked their stock and drove them up to Hope Valley to feed. Another group of people passed through, and Edmund noted a few slaves among them.

Snow began falling as the company crossed the main ridge and drove westward. They passed about fifty oxen and twenty mules under the care of a government officer on his way to aid emigrants who had been stopped by snow east of the mountains. On Saturday, October 13, Edmund wrote in his journal,

> Our distance from the Pass is, by the guide book, 49 miles. Our tired animals travel but slowly. . . . My small . . . ox gave out day before yesterday

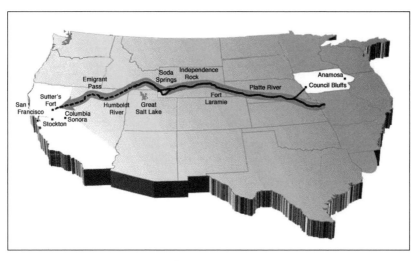

Edmund Booth's journey on the California Trail took just over six months. He stopped in numerous places along the way. This map shows his key stops as well as the California towns where he spent significant time mining for gold. Adapted from a map that appeared in the *San Francisco Chronicle* on August 27, 1998.

and is left 16 miles back. I have but two head left. We are now, by the guide book, distant from "Pleasant Valley," the first gold mines, 12 miles; and from there to Sutter's 55. . . . We shall rejoice to be through, although the soldiers whom we met yesterday do not give so pleasant an account of things in California as did the Mormons in the Great Basin. We have heard nothing from the world at large since we left the Missouri.[28]

After camping near a party of soldiers at Pleasant Valley, Edmund traveled 8 miles to Weaversville. Although it was only a village of a few recently built log cabins and many tents, Edmund enjoyed seeing "civilization" again after so long a journey over desert and desolation. He stayed there about a week, and then traveled on to Sutter's Mill. Two days later he arrived in Sacramento.

On October 25, 1849, Edmund sat down and penned his last note in his California Trail journal: "It was a long journey of nearly six months, a pleasant journey, because of the novelty all along the road, until the last 200 miles, or about that, when the monotony grew rather tiresome."[29]

Tuesday Aug 21 — This morning I put my
cattle (2 yokes) with Hebards team. He
is from Ohio. Clough preferred paddling
his own canoe & cut the down the wagon
to a cart & went on with one yoke —
The wagon not good in the Wheels & axes.
Distance to day (since noon) 12 m
Hebard & Keep — the first from Wisconsin, the 2d from
this is Fort Madison Iowa —

Tues Wednesday Aug 22. Trav? 5 miles & camped
near a high bluff in front of us. 2 or 3 m of the
road along a stream running down the mountains till
it met another from the north & kept on West.
Here we camped. I lay on the ground & slept for
an hour. Some of our teams then went on 4 m further
me & the Jones Co boys stayed; not deeming it
worth while to disturb the animals for 4 m
for fear of being beaten by the St Louis Co
of ox teams which now came up & went
along —

Thursday Aug 23d — Went 4 m along the stream down
Left the stream and traveled a desert plain 13 m
when we struck the Eastern head of Raft River
as we suppose — Went on 4 m further & some

Edmund Booth kept a journal during his six-month journey across the country. He left Anamosa, Iowa, on May 9, 1849, and arrived in California on October 25, 1849. This page, dated August 21–23, 1849, reveals the slow progress of the wagon trains as they headed west. Courtesy of The Haggin Museum, Stockton, California.

FIVE

The Making of a Forty-Niner

EDMUND Booth spent the first few days in the land of gold much as he had along the California Trail. He prepared supper with his companions in the usual way, talked through the evening, spread his blankets on the ground, and slept soundly until morning. One of the first things he did in Sacramento was look for the post office.

> After breakfast, I went for the post office. . . . found it after some inquiry, and asked the postmaster for letters. I stood by his side, as he sorted them, and grabbed at one letter with the name of *Booth*. I had written my name as *E. Booth*. The postmaster held it back and showed it had a different given name. I was greatly disappointed of course. Five months from home, after a journey across deserts and through uncertainties of [a] route unknown. . . . and wife and Tom, seven years old, and Hattie, the baby of one year, all left behind. I had requested wife to write me once or twice and direct to Sacramento City.[1]

In his first letter from California to Mary Ann, Edmund wrote proudly, "I said 'I should come through' and here I am!" He knew that he would have no answer for at least two months or longer. The mail steamers made only monthly trips. He told Mary Ann he would write every month and he hoped that she would do the same. In today's age of pagers and cell phones, one reads his words with especial sympathy. "Do not forget that I must necessarily be *anxious*. . . . in the absence of letters from home, *I have many fears.*"[2]

There were many problems with the mail. Mary Ann had sent several letters to Sacramento while Edmund was on the Plains, but he did not receive them upon his arrival. He constantly watched the posted lists of

53

letters, hoping that his name would appear, but in California the transfer of such correspondence was extremely slow. The Postmaster General had repeatedly issued a general request in the newspapers to discourage the use of sealing wax on letters sent to California. When sealing wax melted, letters would stick together and upon arrival in San Francisco the addresses were often destroyed. Edmund suspected that some letters for him had been lost in that way. He was tired from the long journey, but relieved to have successfully made it. "I am glad you and the children did not come with me," he wrote. "It would have been a bad journey for you and Thomas and would probably kill Harriet."[3]

Shortly after arriving in California, Edmund met a young man who was driving a mule team up the Sacramento River to the diggings and needed assistance. Edmund accepted this opportunity. A few days after they started, the rainy season set in. The rain was at first light, and they slept at night in a tent. But about a week after they had begun the trip, a very heavy rain forced them to let loose the mules on a small island in the river. The next morning they found the island covered and the mules gone. The owner of the team went for help to look for the mules. Edmund never reported what happened to them. He had seen many men going south the past few days and he decided to head that way, traveling until it became dark. It was cloudy and slightly rainy as he started to cross a large wooded region. After a half hour, he found himself where he had started out. He tried again, but without a compass it was fruitless. He took a blanket out of his carpetbag, ate supper, laid his butcher knife by his side and slept soundly in the light rain until broad daylight. In the morning, he began walking again, and after about a half mile, he saw smoke. He walked toward it to find its source.

> It proved to be a small encampment for the night, of a wagon team and three or four men that had been coming south, like myself, the day before. They had kept on the road from which I had turned off. Their wet blankets were hanging before the fire to dry and I followed their example, ate my breakfast of hardtack and soon was at ease among them.[4]

After drying his blankets, Edmund packed up and joined a man from Boston, Massachusetts, well educated, and good-natured, who was headed to Fremont. Edmund told the man that 80,000 people had come over the plains that summer. "His reply was instant: 'I pity the poor devils.'" Edmund, too, wondered what lay in store for so many people who shared the dream of finding gold. "By this time I had learned that gold digging was, with many, a matter of chance."[5]

He and his companion soon reached two adobe houses on the bank of the Sacramento. As the town of Fremont was still miles away, Edmund decided to stop for the night. The young man from Boston went on. Edmund found the door of one of the adobe houses open, so he entered and found four Indians sitting around the fire. He greeted them with the salutation sign and signified a request to stay overnight. John C. Fremont had written that the California Indians were friendly, so Edmund had no fear of them. They indeed welcomed him and Edmund took a seat, drew a few hardtacks from his bag, and offered one to each. In return, the Indians gave Edmund the leg of a deer they had just roasted. Soon all but one of them left. Edmund took out a small bag of Mandrake pills from his sack; the lone Indian understood the use of pills and at once put out his hand for some of them. In his autobiography, Edmund summarized his short stay with the Indians as follows:

> After while and some talk by signs, he motioned me to sleep on the floor, hard earth, enjoy the fire, and left for the other house. I slept soundly. Morning came. Ate my breakfast and went out. In a few seconds a dozen or so Indian men and boys, entirely naked, emerged from the other house and in single file and ran to the river, a few rods away. I followed anxious to see what it all meant. They took a long net from a pole and strung out in line, plunged into the river, swam around and brought in a lot of trout. . . . I shouldered my baggage and resumed my way to the town of Fremont.[6]

Edmund passed a herd of about a hundred wild deer and saw Indians gathering grass and acorns for food. He reached Fremont, which sat on the banks of the Sacramento River, after two or three hours. Passing by shanties, tents, and a boarding house, he found several stores that had a limited supply of groceries brought from such Atlantic ports as New York and Boston. There were no more than 100 inhabitants in the town.

Edmund's legs broke out with scurvy from many months of living on salt provisions. He bought some sauerkraut and ate it ravenously. The water in the river was too high for work, so he stayed in Fremont for several weeks. He earned a few dollars by cutting down some trees and selling a few cords of firewood to a businessman. Soon after arriving in Fremont, he learned that a stern-wheel steamboat stopped there daily. A newspaper agent on board sold New York newspapers that were several weeks old for $.25. Hungry for news and something to read, Edmund bought the papers. The *New York Tribune, Herald,* and one or two other papers also printed special editions for the California market, but these came only once a month. Each paper was not more than four pages, never enough reading for Edmund.

With the health problems he had experienced while at the American Asylum in Hartford years earlier, it is not surprising that Edmund developed a soreness in his lungs while living in the tent and sleeping on the damp ground in his blankets. He searched for a place to stay and found a boarding house run by a family with a deaf child.

> At once I applied to a man who, with his wife, kept a boarding house and was admitted. They were from Illinois and had with them a *deaf mute* daughter eight or ten years of age. . . . I told them to go back to Illinois and place her in the school at Jacksonville and they thought they would. The man and wife were a kindly couple . . . at my request, I desiring nothing more, the woman made me a cup of coffee and I sat on the floor in my blankets, by the stove all night. Better in the morning and after that had a bed and took my meals with the family. In a week, the man sickened and died. The woman broke up housekeeping and I never knew what became of them after that.[7]

It is typical of deaf people to take note of others in their lives who are also deaf. They have an affinity for finding one another, a result of shared experiences, especially the isolation caused by deafness and the challenges of communicating with hearing people. Edmund apparently experienced much less isolation than many deaf people did in his time, and we are left to wonder about the reaction of this young deaf girl in California, having met a deaf man who was the equal of any forty-niner with normal hearing around.

THE water level in the Sacramento River finally fell enough to pan for gold in the river banks. Edmund found good-natured people everywhere. Just as he was about to take the next steamer for Marysville, a friend offered free passage if he would help row a boat up the river. Edmund accepted the offer, but as night approached the wind became too strong for their safety. They went ashore and waited a few hours and resumed when the wind died down. The next day, Edmund shouldered his pack, carpet sack, and blankets, and joined a half dozen men traveling by foot up the banks of Feather River.

Edmund's first mining experience was with a group of men from New Jersey. He and three others dug and wheeled the dirt to a rocker, a device that helped separate gold from dirt. Another man worked the pump to wash the dirt. The two owners had built a shanty and also kept a cook. They lived comfortably, each man receiving $8 a day and free board. "The joke was we received the pay of a congressman and paid out nothing for board and lodgings."[8]

After several weeks, the claim gave out and the owners gave up. With over $100 in gold dust in his pocket, Edmund then started for Marysville by foot again, pack on back as usual. During the few hours' walk, he saw a team of several yoke of oxen and a wagon going up to the mines. As he was about to pass he noticed the driver curiously looking at his face and clothes. It was Clark of Monticello, Iowa, who had been with him on the long journey across the Plains. "My first words, as soon as we had time to recognize one another," he wrote to Mary Ann, "were 'Have you heard from home?' You may judge from this what has been most in my thought since my arrival in this country. Clark has heard nothing from home and we were like hundreds and thousands of others in this respect."[9]

After talking a few minutes they went their own ways. When Edmund reached Marysville, he learned that men were being hired to row another boat to Sacramento City, and he joined eight or ten others the next morning for Reddings Diggings. At noon they stopped at an inn, ate a meal at a half dollar each, and went on to Sacramento City, arriving in the evening. Edmund then decided to go by himself to the southern mines, but he had to wait several days because of rain. He found an ordinary hotel, where, for $2 a day, every man slept in his own blankets on the floor or on benches. Some hotels charged two ounces of gold dust a week for board and lodgings. When the rain stopped, Edmund left with a man from Long Island for Coloma 60 miles away, where gold had been first discovered. As night came, they stopped at a big log still burning, left by previous campers. They ate a supper of crackers, lay down in their blankets, and slept undisturbed.

Coloma, just north of Placerville, included stores, hotels, saloons, gambling houses, and banks. Just outside of town stood the skeleton of Sutter's Mill and below it the race in which James Marshall discovered the gold that brought about the settlement of California. Many of the new emigrants first headed to Coloma, and a bridge had been constructed across the North Fork of the American River to handle the increased traffic.

Edmund slept at the only hotel in Coloma, a two-story building kept by a big-hearted Missouri man who also had left his wife behind to mine for gold. On a large flat nearby, many men were working with picks, shovels, and rockers. The Long Island man had a sheet-iron rocker and the next day the landlord joined them and the three went to work on the flat. They made only a few dollars a day. After a week or so they agreed to go to Placerville. Edmund's Long Island companion shouldered his rocker and Edmund carried the baggage, and after a walk of a few miles they were there. They stayed for several weeks and worked with varying success, making from $2 to $10 per day.

> We were new to the business, and *long toms* and sluices had not come into use. Washing gold by the rocker was slow work. We boarded at the only hotel in the place at $18 a week and slept in our cabin. My companion was an intelligent and genial man. . . . I grew tired of this slow success and concluded to go further south to Sonora, in Tuolumne County, 60 miles east of Stockton.[10]

༺༻

BEFORE leaving Placerville, Edmund traveled briefly to Sacramento City to check for mail from Mary Ann. It was February and he still had not received any news from home. The quintessential pioneering woman,

Mary Ann had been living with family members rather unhappily for about 10 months. After Edmund left for California, she and the two children moved in with Henry Booth. Fairview had only a half dozen log cabins and frame houses at the time. The school was located in the basement of Dr. Matson's large, frame house, and the local children were taught by Miss Aletha Hall.

From the start, Mary Ann suffered the loss of her independence. She desperately wished to cook, sew, and raise the children without her relatives around. Throughout the years Edmund was in California, and afterwards, she demonstrated great self-reliance. She did not need, or desire, assistance. She took the seeds of a tasty apple and produced trees that supplied the family with applesauce for years. She invested $90 in 5 acres of farmland and told her children in sign language that a day would arrive when someone would offer much more for that same land. She deftly curled young Hattie's hair for a daguerreotype photograph, and made beautiful clothes for the children from homespun yarn. She planned for planting, harvesting, and selling crops, raising cattle, and she dealt with the fencing and clearing of land and other business matters associated with the family farm. A devoted wife and mother, she was well suited for single handedly raising two children—a role thrust upon her by Edmund's departure for the California gold mines.

For five years Mary Ann filled her days with the formidable challenges of raising a family in a suddenly and profoundly altered environment. But as a woman who was deaf and did not speak, she was marginalized by family, friends, and strangers. They questioned her abilities and sometimes took advantage of her lack of experience in financial affairs. She was extremely patient, but understandably frustrated. Mary Ann's writing is less eloquent than Edmund's, at times showing the nuances of having been deaf since an early age, but her intelligence and fortitude were responsible for a happy and healthy family that largely prevailed during Edmund's mining years. Her letters reveal her struggles and bravery as a frontierswoman; her fears were mingled with tears, and, at times anger, but she always hoped for Edmund's safe return.

Mary Ann had indeed sent Edmund several letters, but they had not reached him in California by the time she received his letter on January 2, 1850. She had directed her first letter to San Francisco and two others to Sutter's Fort. She wasted no time in responding to him the following day.

> Dear Edmund,
>
> Last night I received your interesting letter. I thank God that you arrived in the gold region safely and I am very glad that your long and tedious journey is ended. . . . I was most crazy for joy to hear that you were well. While I read it, all boarders and children stood around me and watched and felt anxious to know what had become of you, till I finished to read it. I gave it to Durham to read it to them aloud. . . . Mr. Skinner asked me if I was not glad that I did not go with you and I answered no. He laughed. I told him if I had no children I would like to go with you and see the country.[11]

Mary Ann mentioned that she had read in the newspapers about 500 emigrants who became discouraged and returned home. She asked Edmund if he were disappointed not to find enough gold. Even in this letter, she was anxious about when he would be returning home, following with an expression of hope "that we will be happy to live better in the future when you get rich."[12]

Friends in Iowa were also curious about Benjamin Clough, Edmund's deaf friend who had accompanied him on the overland journey. "They wondered why you did not say a word about Clough and believe that he might be dead. The people here heard that I had a letter from you and felt anxious to inquire about you and Clough. . . . They liked him very well because he had great friends here."[13] Edmund subsequently explained to Mary Ann that he had left Clough in Weaverstown and had not heard from him since.[14]

In her January 3 letter, Mary Ann also described the local schoolteacher, Miss Hall, who arranged for four sleighs to take the children for a ride and followed this event with a party. "She said Thomas was a good singer. Miss Hall told me that he was learning very fast and he would make the first rate scholar."[15] Mary Ann wished Edmund a happy new year and told him about some decisions she had made regarding the family finances, including selling the old cow for $12 to pay taxes. Thomas often encouraged her to write and she was proud that he could read as well as Hannah's son William.

※§℘※

ON MARCH 19, 1850, Edmund expressed delight over finally receiving Mary Ann's earlier letters, as well as other correspondence.

> Sunday, I went to an express office and obtained two letters one from you dated Dec. 2nd. The other from George in [New Orleans]: date Nov. 13th. I felt much relieved for I had not heard one word from home since I left in May—over ten months.[16]

It had been only a few months since he arrived in California and already he was planning his return. "I intend to start for home at the beginning of the rainy season in November." He was considering going by way of Panama, possibly returning in the spring the same way. Although his boredom with farming was part of the reason he left Iowa, he wrote to her that "I would rather however be on my farm than be gold digging." Edmund had not used a razor nor cut any of this hair since he was near Fort Laramie. "In this matter," he wrote to Mary Ann, "I am a match for old Jupiter."[17] Edmund's next letter indicates that he was missing his children: "I suppose by this time Harriet can run about and probably has forgotten her papa entirely." He predicted that California would one day be "well enough for families to come, but it needs heroines to make the beginning." He still expected to start for home in the fall; nevertheless, he warned Mary Ann that "I will not till I get enough to greatly improve our circumstances."[18]

As the summer of 1850 approached, mining became difficult. During the summer, or dry season, the mines could be worked only where water was in streams or was brought through the ditches. The water levels in the rivers were too high. The dry season forced work to stop on many good claims. By mid-August, Edmund appeared to be contemplating a longer stay. He remained optimistic, writing to Mary Ann that should he spend any portion of the coming rainy season in this part of the country, "I shall hardly fail of doing well. In the river (Tuolumne) on which I am now located I expect to make fifteen hundred at the least before the rainy season opens. Most men say they expect to make from three to five thousand, and I may do that."[19]

Miners often worked in groups, sharing the work and the claims. They dug canals at various points along the river and built dams in order to leave the middle of the river bare for mining. Had Edmund arrived three or four months earlier, he could have had a share in one of the canals. One particular canal opposite Jacksonville took over 100 days to dig, and cost each shareholder over $1000. Edmund was offered a half share for $1000, but he did not accept.[20] Without access to one of the canals, he and two other men were forced to mark off a 6-foot-square claim on the riverbank, which was then under water. They waited about fifteen days for the river to turn so they could work on it.

Edmund was usually realistic on the subject of making money. He often explained to Mary Ann the uncertainty involved—"A few men make hundreds or thousands in a few hours or a few days; while the many require months to accomplish the same object—this is the general feature throughout California." About the claim he was working on, he told her, "We may make much and may make nothing on it."[21]

Edmund warned Mary Ann not to believe the newspaper stories about lumps of gold weighing 80 or 90 pounds. "We know they are false, but these stories, got up by traders, merchants and speculators to get more fools into the country accomplish their purpose to a certain extent— witness the immense immigration across the deserts this year. They will suffer sadly." He also told her that California was no place for men who could not take care of themselves.

> It is well enough for poor men without families to come dig for gold, but if a man is doing well, living comfortably . . . if he takes a notion to leave his family & come to California, I would advise Rockwell, as County Attorney, to have him indicted forthwith as *non compos mentis* and incapable of taking care of himself. About one third of the men here have families in the East. Some say nothing, but most complain . . . of the separation and the long uncertainty between the receipt of letters. Most of the men here are from

Massachusetts & Rhode Island. . . . Over one hundred within 12 miles are from New Bedford.[22]

Edmund had been in California for 10 months, and had received only one packet of letters from home. He wrote to Mary Ann of his disappointment and his desire to come home: "the last letter I had from you was of date Jan. 3rd—seven months ago. A paper afterwards, marked Feb. 13th, I rec'd in May. Such is a part of life in California. . . . I shall be glad to be at home again. There is no place like home, and I am weary of this wandering life. It is restless and unsatisfactory."[23]

☙❧❧

BACK home in Iowa, Mary Ann and the children were having an eventful summer of 1850. At one point, she and Thomas joined a wagonload of family and friends, including Edmund's sister, Hannah, and her children, Maria, William, and Harlow, for a day of blackberry picking west of Fairview. Julius and J. M. Peet, Ambrose and Neal Parsons, and others had opened up prairie farms along a section of timber stretching for miles east to west. Mary Ann, always independent and sometimes obstinate, often went off in her own direction. On this day, the other berry pickers went west along the Parsons Way, while Mary Ann and Thomas took the Fairview road directly east. They walked along the heavy timber, mostly great white oaks, and turned northward into a valley of dense undergrowth, where they found a large patch of berries. Within an hour they had wandered apart and out of sight of each other. Thomas looked up and down the hollow, realizing there was no way to call out for his deaf mother. He tramped up and down and over the hills and back again, always fearing wildcats. Finally, terror-stricken, he started for home, taking the path that led to the highway. He walked west toward Mrs. Olmstead's log cabin, a quarter of a mile east from Fairview, and then on to his Uncle Henry's house, a distance of probably one mile altogether. He imagined his mother frantically searching for him, similarly fearing wildcats and rattlesnakes. Fortunately, Mary Ann also found her way back.[24]

During that same summer, Hattie was knocked unconscious in a fall while playing. She at first appeared dead, but she was revived. Thomas, too, had a narrow escape when he was thrown from a wagon at his Uncle Henry's place. The oxen had suddenly started forward, and the quick thinking of a friend, who pulled him aside, possibly saved Tom's life.

As time passed, Mary Ann grew increasingly upset about living with relatives. In the early fall, when Henry Booth began working at Gideon Ford's hotel, the Wapsipinicon House, she and the children had to move into the hotel. They were now living with two of Edmund's siblings.

❧❦❧

IN THE fall of 1850, Edmund sent Mary Ann three-fourths of an ounce of gold from the Tuolumne River at Jacksonville. He explained that the gold there was being dug up as both fine dust and in lumps washed down the river from the mountains. He put the gold in a cloth to prevent the lumps from breaking holes through the paper, but he feared that the letter would be lost or stolen because of its weight. "What is here is a sample of the dry diggings," he wrote to her. "It is the same in the river with the addition of more fine dust. You can use it as you please." Edmund explained that if the gold was not bright she should throw it into water and shake it. California gold was not as yellow as gold coins because it also contained silver. He had seen both pure silver and quicksilver in lumps of gold, as well as quartz in some of the lumps. He told Mary Ann that "these make no difference with us in regard to value."[25] He planned to send a larger quantity of gold to San Francisco and then have a reliable company forward her a bank draft, which she could exchange for money. He would keep a duplicate of the draft. If the one he sent to Mary Ann was stolen, he explained, it would be of no use unless endorsed by her.

Along the banks of the river, Edmund saw many of the men who accompanied him to California. Success was not yet very great for most of them, including himself. "I have made as much as $11.50 a day, he wrote."[26] The days were still very hot, but the nights were growing cool and the "more delicate" men put on their coats in the evening. In a week or so, regular and steady work would commence for many miles along the river, and such work would continue until stopped by the rainy weather in November. By now it was certain that he was postponing his return to Iowa. He had not earned enough to make the trip worthwhile and maintained hope that in time he would do so. He predicted that in a month or so he would probably be in some of the winter diggings at or near Sonora, 12 miles away.

> I suppose, from seeing with my own eyes, there is gold enough in these mountains to sink a whole navy of the United States. But to dig it is another affair. The people of the U.S. and the speculators and merchants in California are insane on the subject. The only people who are in their senses are the diggers. Calif. is now flooded with provisions and goods of all kinds and competition in everything is keen. The result is many failures; and those who don't fail must be content with moderate gains.[27]

Edmund called himself a "wandering exile." He must have wondered at times about how safe it would be for a deaf man to walk around in the dark. Had a guard called out to him to stop, he would have been unable to heed the warning and could have been shot. He was staying at a hotel, paying $14 per week for room and board. The miners had plenty of food—local gardens supplied cabbage, potatoes, and tomatoes; raisins sold at the mines far up in the mountains for "their weight in gold dust," fresh beef was abundant, arriving regularly from Mexico, and bushels of pears were brought in from Mexico on the backs of mules. The pears were about the size of black walnuts and sold eight for one dollar. Edmund was not impressed with California as farm country, however. He told Mary Ann that "Iowa is worth a hundred Californias for farming."[28]

With great candor, Edmund shared with Mary Ann his hopes and dreams, his successes and disappointments, and his heartfelt emotions as he struggled to realize his modest goal of bringing home $3,000 to $5,000 for his family. That was all he hoped to earn and he never lost track of his priorities. "I shall rejoice to be at home again," he wrote. "My old log cabin and farm have far more charms for me than all the gold of Cal. and every man who is not a born miser says the same of himself." His motivation for staying was his children.

They must have as good an education as possible, for ignorance and folly usually go together. But I would much prefer to see them honest and kind-hearted than rich. Without honesty and goodness at heart, wealth will do little towards making them happy in life.[29]

Edmund also frequently updated Mary Ann on his health, as he had done on his overland journey. To treat boils on his knee, he wrapped it with a cold, wet towel three times a day. "Many men in this country cure by cold water and have books on that subject. When unwell, I take a bath, drink plenty of cold water and sleep it off. Have taken no medicine save a little rhubarb."[30]

On September 11, he left Hawkins Bar and crossed the mountains 8 miles to Jacksonville.

[I was] in no very pleasant mood of mind but in hopes of a letter from home. Well, I arrived; but as it was so long (eight or nine months) since my last dates from home, I was almost afraid to inquire, fearful of bad news. So I sat down in the express office and read the papers[;] in about fifteen minutes the principal of the house came in and at once brought me the list of letters with his finger at my name. I sprang up and ran into the office where he gave me your letter of May 22nd. Its reading raised my spirits 100 degrees. If you knew the value of letters to me in this strange land you would write more frequently—at least once a month.[31]

His disappointments in mining were overcome in part by the loving support he found in her correspondence. "With time and labor lost and my expectations blasted, I returned to Hawkin's Bar in better spirits (from being assured that all were well at home) than I had possessed for some two or three weeks previous." But he also wrote that his dog, Towser, "would [have been] some consolation in this my banishment. I never see a dog but I think of Towser."[32] Edmund does not say what became of Towser, but, in later years, Thomas recalled that his father told him the dog gradually dropped behind the wagons on the California Trail, and eventually failed to come up to their wagon.

A year had gone by, but Edmund was unable to help Mary Ann financially in any significant way. "You had better rent the farm," he advised her on November 3, 1850. "Rent it on shares if it is still the custom. In my last [letter] I stated that I was intending to send you something. My connection with the damming Co. nearly emptied my pocket, for board was $15 per week and a set of tools will cost over $50. You must wait a little longer."[33]

In the same letter Edmund responded to Mary Ann's request to come to California with an adamant

> *No.* I will never consent to you and the children taking so dangerous a journey in the care of others. On the road along the Humboldt and after, men were left dead and dying, uncared for, for nearly all were weak and starving and all fearing to share the same fate. When I came, the immigrants were overloaded with provisions . . . and the Humboldt was not overflowed. This year everything was on the other extreme. [34]

Then he offered the following sage advice to Henry Booth and Gideon Ford, who were thinking of coming the following spring.

> That two such cautious, prudent and sensible men are so badly bitten shows the intensity of the California fever in the East. It makes me laugh. But if I was required to give a decisive *yes* or *no* to their coming I should say *yes*, with the remark that if they have a good prospect of getting along well where they are, they had best remain. They will soon know if they do not know already that thousands have left Cal. without making their "pile." Few out of the many make fortunes. Experience teaches men to be content with half an ounce a day. If they do better they are lucky. I have heard of two men taking out forty thousand in one week, but such cases are extremely rare.[35]

Edmund's diary and his correspondence with Mary Ann frequently made mention of communicating by "signs." He likely meant the gestures most hearing people he encountered used to communicate with him. In the case of business dealings with the miners or evening chats at the campfires, the conversations recorded in his journal include remarkable detail. However, the journal also reveals that many of his exchanges in "signs" were simple forms of conveying basic wants, needs, or other messages, as the following two examples show:

I invariably unconsciously passed far ahead, stopped and waited for them [two Chinese men] to come up. On reaching me they both told me in urgent signs to not go ahead but to keep by them. I inferred they were afraid of being attacked and robbed, for we passed now and then a traveller or team coming from the mines.

On one occasion I met a Mexican. Kept an open eye on him as he was about to pass. He stopped suddenly and spoke. I made the sign of not being able to hear. He understood and pointed to his open mouth, meaning he wanted food. I swung around my pack, took out three or four big square crackers and gave him. He looked hungry. As he took the crackers he made the sign of the cross, pointed slightly upward and then to me. I interpreted it to mean, "The Holy Virgin bless you." It was rather a pleasant adventure and I sat down to see what he would do on meeting my Chinese friends. He passed them with no sign. When they came up they scolded me in their way for going so fast. It was evident they regarded me as a protection to them.[36]

In all of Edmund's writings, there is little mention of his ability to speechread (lipread). He must have had limited but intelligible speech, for how else would he have been able to converse with so many different people?

ॐ ९ ९ ॐ

EDMUND'S first year in California ended with one more discouraging event. He was offered a half share in a damming company on the condition that he work until the dam was finished. After nearly two weeks of the most laborious work he had ever performed, heavy rains destroyed or damaged every dam on the river. The company members waited a week for the water level to drop and then decided to hold the work until spring. Instead, they built two temporary coffer dams, but the first dam was on ground too high, and the second one, in the middle of the river, could not withstand the pressure of the water. They were forced to abandon it.

Edmund read in the Sacramento City newspapers that similar misfortunes had happened in the northern mines. Some of the dams were repaired. To make things worse, at Hawkins' Bar he saw two rockers take out $3,000 in a single afternoon from a spot 3-feet long, 1-foot wide, and

6- or 8-inches deep. He wrote to Mary Ann from Sonora on November 3, summarizing his travails with the dams and the difficult and heart-wrenching decision he had to make:

> Probably you are thinking that I am now on my way home; and so, in Sept. last, I expected to be; and doubtless should be had the fates been propitious. Alas! it was otherwise; and I am now in Cal. for another winter. . . . It was a most bitter disappointment all along. We had all expected to make our thousands and go home this Autumn.[37]

He also missed the children. "I often wish Thomas was with me," he wrote. "That would be something like home; but the mining country is no place for boys. He could do nothing, while there is a vast amount of bad talking and no schools at all."[38]

SIX

Best Friends

𖤘𖤘

EDMUND Booth's correspondence in 1851 focused on gold mining, his daily routines, his advice to Mary Ann on raising the family, and his counsel to friends back home who were thinking of coming to California. He told Mary Ann in January that he was doing only "tolerably well" with his mining. "You are not however to suppose that I am in despair, going to shoot or hang myself or that I am even discouraged," he wrote. "I know the mines too well for the last named feeling to take possession of me. My greatest annoyance is the absence of rain—Water for washing out the dust."[1]

In early January he went alone to Camp Seco on a prospecting tour. Over the next two weeks he pulled in from $.50 to $18 a day, averaging about $5. He told Mary Ann about men in the southern mines who made $4 to $8 per day; yet he knew other men who worked day after day and barely made expenses. He wished he had been there a year earlier. "The best places so far as known are dug out, exhausted; and the mines are not so enormously profitable as they have been. Still a man by perseverance can make a good sum in the course of a few months or a year or two."[2]

Perseverance was indeed a feature of his personality. He would not acquiesce to the sometimes maddening failure to find the gold he sought. Certainly, he was earning more than he would have as a teacher in Anamosa, where teacher's salaries were the same as they had been when he had left Hartford twelve years earlier. His earnings from farming would have been little better. Yet, the prospects for mining appeared to be diminishing as the scale of operations expanded. Individual miners like Edmund experimented with placer mining, river mining, and hydraulic mining in an attempt to maintain their independence, but they sometimes had to resort to working for wages. Like many other men, Edmund stayed in California partly because his financial prospects were even lower at home. With each shovelful of dirt came that neverending hope of getting rich, but the reality of the Gold Rush had become painfully obvious to him. His words of advice to those back home thinking of making the long trek to California were "that unless they can keep sober whether in prosperity or adversity and can bear up under difficulties and disappointments, they had better go and hang themselves than start for Cal."[3]

Edmund was a man who recognized the unpredictable nature of those around him, yet he always seemed to focus on the positive, often translating his experiences in life to meaningful lessons for his children. Even at a distance of thousands of miles, he endeavored to educate young Thomas, at first through Mary Ann, and later by direct correspondence with his son. In a January letter, he wrote:

> I am glad that the children and you all are well and of your assurance that Thomas is a good boy. I am more anxious about them than about anything else. I hope they will grow up with feelings of truth, justice and humanity. We see too little of these qualities in the world. But still there are some men who carry them out in daily practice and these are worth all the rest of the world around them.[4]

His correspondence frequently focused on human nature and his value of human life. He was willing to offer advice to friends back home about how to pack the wagons and transverse the deserts, but his greatest fear was that the journey would cost them their lives. The self-destructive behaviors and bullying of some miners were a challenge to the generally gentle man. Edmund occasionally met men who tried to cheat him out of his claims. At one particular claim, the miner adjacent to him pulled up the stake and moved it some feet into Edmund's claim. Edmund moved it back, but the other miner moved it once again. This back-and-forth moving continued for a while. Finally, Edmund responded to a belligerent movement by the other man by striking him on the cheek with a long-handled shovel. The burly deaf man had settled the argument and there was no further hostility. Edmund rarely was involved in violence of any kind during his entire stay in California, and he did not even record this incident in his journal. Rather, his son Thomas later described it based on his father's recollections after his return to Iowa. Edmund was generally a gentle man who valued his relationships with others. "Here in California," he wrote to Mary Ann in January 1851, "I find good men as well as bad; and somehow or other I always have friends among the good."[5]

Edmund sent Mary Ann and Thomas each a book as Christmas and New Year's presents. He would have sent one to Harriet, but books for children were difficult to find in California. "For the same reason Julia [his niece] must wait for her ring—ladies are very scarce in the mountains and of course the traders do not bring rings for them."[6]

While he worked in the southern mines Edmund lived in a boarding house kept by two black men from Florida and a young Mexican. He slept in his blankets on the bare ground, rose before the sun, rolled up and threw the blankets into a corner and, as the sun rose, sat down to breakfast before going to work one-half mile below the town. After working all day, he cleaned his gold, threw it into a tin box, put it into one of the pockets of his miner's coat, and went into town.

> My pantaloons (over my boots) are at such times covered to the knees with a thick coating of mud and I am splashed from head to foot. But there is no clean water wherewith to wash my face. So I go directly to the Florida House for the purpose. Having done that, I sit down by the fire—put the tin box on the coals and in a few minutes the gold is dry. Then going to the counter I weigh it and thereby know the result of my day's work—putting the gold into my purse. I go out to the express office and read the papers or sit and dry my pants at the fire. The evening passes in reading, talking, thinking of home . . . or as I am now—writing.[7]

It had not rained for nearly a month, and more than 50,000 miners scattered the whole length of California were

> praying for rain or growling and even swearing at the want of it. Every morning as I rise, and every evening before I throw myself on my hard bed, I look anxiously at the sky. This scarcity of rain will cause the loss of millions

of dollars to the miners, for immense quantities of dirt have been dug up to be washed this winter. The first rain that enabled us to wash did not fall till after the 20th of Nov. During the present week [the third week of January] I have been throwing up dirt as have many others and have hopes of rain almost daily, as for some days past clouds have been floating in the sky.[8]

Edmund hoped the California gold fever had passed its climax and was on the decline.[8] Those who came first had made out best. He believed that no family should come to California unless they intended to settle permanently in the country. "I am inclined," he wrote to Mary Ann, "to bring you all here some years hence and settle as a farmer near San Jose or South of the Bay or near Vallejo (in Napa Valley) north of the Bay. This winter climate is decidedly beautiful and no labor required to keep animals from dying of cold or starvation." For the time being, though, he was determined to stay: "My wish is to make from three to five thousand. How long it will take is uncertain. One man lately took out near Sonora eighteen pounds in a day (about $3,500)."[9]

Edmund told Mary Ann that he had found a lump worth $4.25, which he sent her. The same day a Mexican found a lump weighing four pounds worth about $800. He also described the excitement in Sonora over a new discovery of a vein of gold in quartz rock. The veins, however, could not be worked without expensive machinery. He asked Mary Ann who among the neighbors was coming to California that spring.

They should be accustomed to labor and to habits of temperance and possess resolution enough to bear up under disappointments for every man here meets with a thousand such. For instance, he spends several days in sinking a hole for gold and in the end finds nothing. In such case his only remedy is to try again in another place. An indomitable perseverance is a necessary qualification in a gold hunter.[10]

Edmund emphasized that the emigrants should bring plenty of potatoes and eat them freely. Medical writers and chemists claimed that the potato was a good source of potash, which would prevent scurvy. Every man should bring a bushel, at least fifty pounds of sugar, as well as flour, meat, beans, coffee, dried apples, and a small quantity of vinegar. He told

Mary Ann that an appetite on the deserts is like that of a wolf. He sent her the December 1, 1850, *Stockton Journal*, which contained a more truthful account of the yield of the mines and more honest advice to those at home who were thinking of coming to California. When Edmund's nephew, Danforth, asked him if he should come to California, Edmund counseled against it. He did not think Danforth was old enough or accustomed to severe labor. Edmund had given the same advice to Thomas. If his son wished to know what mining was like, he should take a shovel and excavate a mass of red sand, clay, and rocks near the military road. If, after a week's continuous labor, from sunrise to sunset, stopping only for an hour each day for dinner, Thomas did not complain of an aching back, weary limbs, or feel his spirit changing for the worse, then perhaps he would be fit for California.

༄༅

IN THE spring of 1851, Mary Ann and the children moved out of the Wapsipinicon Hotel and in first with Linus Osborn and then with Lewis Perkins and his family after the Osborn residence was damaged by a flood. She earned some money for herself by washing and making clothing. Edmund was sympathetic over Mary Ann's displeasure about living with family members. "If you wish," he wrote in February, "you can perhaps rent a small house or a set of rooms and live by yourselves. It will not, I think, cost much; and in so orderly a town as Anamosa you will suffer no annoyance."[11]

Mary Ann did not receive the books and letters Edmund sent in January and February until April. One evening Lewis Perkins returned from the post office with a book for Mary Ann. She sat down to read it after supper while Perkins went to the post office again to wait for the other mail from Chicago. She was reading when he came in with mail from Edmund.

> Before I had read two pages, I was interrupted by opening the door. Perkins came in and smiled at me, I understood and started from my chair . . . and caught your letters which I was in a hurry to open with trembling feelings for I feared that there were bad news in them; but I found all good news

from you. I read your long and interesting letters three times. I never got tired of reading any of your letters.[12]

Mrs. Perkins was difficult to live with. She apparently did not enjoy having children around and sometimes made Harriet cry. Meanwhile, a widow named Mrs. Finch had been living on the Booth farm with a child, and although Edmund preferred not to evict her, he left the decision to Mary Ann. His sister Hannah also appeared to be exerting control over Mary Ann's life, despite the fact they were no longer living together. Mary Ann wrote to Edmund that Hannah "came and told me that I must go and see justice of the peace to get a warrant against Mrs. Finch to leave our house immediately."[13] Whether or not Mary Ann was aware of her legal recourses, her letters indicate that she was pressured by relatives to see the constable.

Despite these difficulties, Mary Ann time and again demonstrated her self-sufficiency in financial affairs, in planting, harvesting, and selling crops, and, most importantly, in raising two children. She was tired of living with others and missed her independence so she planned to rent a small house for $2 or $3 a month. She also negotiated with a man named Livermore to rent the Booth farm and repair and split some 500 rails to replace the base rails that were rotten. He would share with her one-third of the crops ready to husk and one-fourth of the grains ready to thrash. She told him she wanted to buy back their old cow for $12 to $15.[14]

Hattie was now nearly three years old and Thomas was nine. Mary Ann often wrote about how the children were growing.

Harriet is . . . very fond of playing with a doll with which she is steady to play daily. When she goes to bed she cries for her doll so I gave it to her which she put on her arm with heartily laugh and joy. I kiss her and leave her alone in the bed. A few minutes after I went to the bed to look at her again, she fell asleep so sweetly with her dolly hugged close to her. I kissed her again gently. I wish you could see her and her rosy cheeks and how she looks innocent and beautiful.[15]

Mary Ann felt bad that Edmund was sleeping on the floor. She also cautioned him to be careful with his gold.

Be careful not to show so much gold to the miners for the danger of being robbed and murdered for your wife's sake and take care of yourself particularly when you are on your way for home, dont talk about gold with the strangers, passengers, nor tell them where you come from. When you arrive here you must be careful not to tell our folks and neighbors how much you shall have made. . . . Some people of Iowa returned from California last winter and would not say anything about how much they had made. I suppose that they were afraid of being robbed or murdered.[16]

She noted that many men, women, and children passed through Anamosa on their way to California and concluded one letter by telling Edmund that she was willing to go West if that were his wish. She was especially interested in what she had read about Oregon—"the country is beautiful, healthy and agreeable for us in the winter." She put pills in his old skin pouch and sent it to him again. "You will laugh at it. I wish I could put myself in this letter and go to Cal. to see you but oh dear I am too large to fold myself up in this small sheet."[17]

Thomas wrote a few lines to his father, including an offer to come to California and help mine for gold and a report that "Harriet is very pleasant some times with deaf Mary and me." Mary Ann added, "Please answer his letter, he will be pleased very much with your letter. I expect another letter from you in May. I will answer it immediately."[18]

⁂

EDMUND'S letters often included long and detailed descriptions of his experiences. He wrote to Mary Ann on April 27, while sitting in a room in Sonora that served as the express office, barroom, billiard room, and justice's office. He had just gotten a bank draft for $200 from Reynolds and Company (Express Agents) and again assured her that it was a safe procedure. "Should you not receive the draft, let me know and I will forward you the duplicate. If stolen it will be worthless, as it will not be complete till endorsed by yourself; and if endorsed by others the act would be forgery and the parties liable to State Prison—forgery being always heavily punished."[19]

The rainy season of 1851 began in earnest and continued for a month. The rain enabled him to work to great advantage and he continued to make about $8 to $10 per day. The largest amount he had made in any one day was $31. He was temporarily struck with hope again. "I shall keep at work till I go home. I cannot say when that will be. I may remain here—a year longer and may find a big lump or a rich lead and be off."[20]

On Sunday afternoons, men thronged into Sonora filling the streets from the north to the south end (a full mile). A Mexican circus or bullfight was always in town. Edmund never attended these events. "The sorry ponies and mules which they ride do not give me any high idea of their *artistic* powers." Although in an earlier letter he had expressed concern about farming in California, he found himself weighing 218 pounds, having gained 38 pounds since his arrival. "Cal. is a great country," he wrote this time with a sense of humor, "not only for growing vegetables but *humans*."[21]

Edmund carefully followed his wife's challenges back home. This was not an easy task with months elapsing between letters. He discussed the house and farm with her, although many of the decisions she made were independent of his counsel, which was not always timely. He agreed with her decision to rent the farm to Mr. Livermore, and the terms she described were all satisfactory. He felt too distant and encouraged her to manage these matters. Although in one letter Mary Ann had requested that he not send another draft, he thought it better to send the money so that she could buy a good frame house or cottage in Anamosa and live in it—"just as you wish."

Get a good [house] on high ground that you may have a dry cellar & be as much as possible away from the fogs, fleas, fever & ague of the marshes. It will give a better chance of health. By buying the house (buy the lot also on which it stands) the money will not be lost, as it will sell again at any time. You will have offers enough, for men will sell anything. Some even their own souls, for gold—and the draft will be as good as that. So if you don't like the first offers, you need not hurry. If you have more money afterwards than you need, let Henry have some. I owe him for your and the children's board and I wish to do something to help Mother. Do not lend under the circumstances. You can always get things more to your liking by having the cash in your pocket.[22]

On May 4, 1851, a terrible fire swept through San Francisco. It burned for 10 hours, destroying an estimated 1,500 to 2,000 houses in 18 blocks of the main business district. As a result of that fire, every newspaper office except one (the *Alta California*) was destroyed. Edmund was cut off from news of the outside world.[23]

Anamosa had its own calamity around the same time—a great flood. Water rushed through town in a stream 50-feet wide. Several houses were destroyed and the town was an island. Linus Osborn's house was among those flooded, which precipitated Mary Ann's move in with the Perkins family. Thomas nearly drowned while swimming in the river with three friends. Coincidentally, Edmund warned his wife in his June 8 letter to be cautious about letting Thomas swim. "You must be careful; and not allow Thomas to bathe in deep water. It will be perhaps some years before he can swim well. He must begin in shallow water. At least where the water is not higher than his head. Boys are drowned every summer for want of this precaution."[24]

Edmund was joyous that he had received a batch of letters from Hannah, Julia, Thomas, Danforth, and Mary Ann. "This is glorious to one so far from home and so far beyond [the] other side of sundown." He wished they would all write him every month. He especially encouraged the children to write because they "have more time, as they have abundant time for their amusements, and they are usually more minute in their statements than older persons, and hence they give me more information. Besides it will accustom them to the use of the pen & putting their thoughts and impressions on paper; and they will find the benefit hereafter." Edmund assured Mary Ann that he would "not criticise their letters very severely, as there is much that can be learned only by reading and practice, but there is one thing which needs only to be pointed out to be mended, and is simply this—to begin a sentence or the name of a person or place with a capital letter—also the first personal pronoun singular. I hope this will not frighten them and prevent their writing. Let them write on freely, as they would speak."[25]

In this same letter, Edmund advised Mary Ann to hire someone to help in getting wood or in any other work. He also told her to buy a house and have it fixed if necessary so that it would be comfortable. He suggested that she go on a shopping excursion with his sister Hannah to get a good cooking stove, "luxuries, a barrel of dried apples, ets." He asked Mary Ann to take the children to a daguerreotypist for a family photograph; he also wanted a picture of his mother.[26]

Edmund still believed in animal magnetism, as did his brother and sister. He suspected that when Thomas was taken ill, the doctor had, without intending it, thrown "the magnetic field (electricity) from his own full charged brain into that of Thomas' which contained little." He recommended that Mary Ann allow Thomas to be magnetized by Hannah or Henry if the boy had "fits."[27]

Writing in the express office at the justice's desk with the barkeeper dealing out liquor on his right and other men sitting at a table reading papers and playing billiards, Edmund described to Mary Ann his dreams of obtaining a farm in the Napa Valley on the north side of the Bay near Vallejo. With its "perpetual summer," even in the mountains, gardens were kept in constant cultivation. Full-grown turnips, lettuce, radishes, and beets were on the table daily. The frosts of California seemed to have no effect on vegetation.[28]

🙟🙠🙚

DESPITE Edmund's upbeat mood about California, Mary Ann was disappointed when she read his June letter. She wrote back to him that she had "expected to find some words in your last letters that *you* were *coming home*."[29] That same month she purchased 5 acres of land from J. H. Fisher for $90. Thomas later recalled his mother's wisdom in buying this land: "She had large visions of the future, and I remember how picturesquely she signed it out, that some time a man would come and take one thousand dollars out of his pocket—please imagine her oratorical air—and hand it over to us for that five acres!"[30]

A man named John Handy learned that Mary Ann wanted a new house on that land, and he came to see her about building it. There was currently no lumber available because the logs at the mills had been swept away by a flood. Handy asked for $150 to build the house. "He is frank and honest and a Christian," Mary Ann explained to Edmund. "I have not money enough to pay for building, but only 100 dollars now; he says he will take one hundred dollars now for building till I can get fifty dollars for him."[31]

Always economical, she complained in this same letter that the postage for the correspondence was too expensive. Edmund's last letter had cost $1.60. She went to the post office to see the postmaster about it, and he explained that there was an express charge on it and the letter was torn. She was angry at having to pay for a letter that contained nothing. "I shall be glad when my home is done," she wrote. "I wish that you can get rich at once so you are coming home. I dreamed often that you came back and that I embraced and kissed you and that I told you that I was very happy to see you, but when I awoke and found myself in bed and you in California!"[32] Mary Ann pleaded with Edmund to consider returning home:

> If you are not coming back next winter I shall live lonesome in our new house in all the gloomy winter; my tears start in my eyes and fall down my cheeks while I am writing, for I think that you will never come back and that you will say that you will stay in Cal. every other year. I did not answer your letters immediately, I received them on thirty first of July, because I felt very discouraged, that you were not coming home. I read Californian papers that the miners are greatly discouraged and could not get rich enough as they expected before they went to Cal. . . . It will keep you long away in Cal. . . . You dont know how I wish that you would be here. I rather die if you dont come back soon.[33]

Mary Ann wanted Edmund to come home not only because she missed him but because she was raising their children alone.

I am so trouble to take care of our children greatly. Thomas is growing [bigger, bigger]. He troubles me greatly for he disobeys and wont mind me what I advise him to take care of himself and I tell him thousand times that he must not be rude to go into the river often a week, for I am afraid that he would be dangerously drowned, before he can learn how to swim, but he [ignored] me, so I whipped him. Harriet is growing fast, she can run about the streets rudely, it worries me all time. I can not keep both of them about home. I wish that I can live in the country which is safer for them, than in the town. They learn [from] the bad children who swear. Julia told me that Thomas often swears. I am very sorry for it. I am afraid that he will become bad and be in bad habit of swearing. I am sorry that I can not hear him done so. . . . I wish that you will write that he must not swear again.

I hope that Thomas will be a good boy again when we shall live in our new house about half mile from this town. I shall give him good books and interesting stories to read often. He can not be steady to read here, for many children are playing around him, and calling him to play with them. There is no help for him to read. I can not wait for him to write a few lines in this letter, for he writes so slow. I must finish this letter this evening, it will go tomorrow morning.[34]

Mary Ann, Thomas, and Hattie moved into their new house in the fall of 1851. Shortly after settling there, Hattie found her mother crying and asked what was wrong. Mary Ann replied that she missed her husband and when Hattie asked why she didn't write and tell him to come home, her mother responded that she had done that and it was no use. Hattie later reminisced about "the days of anxiety and fear and the loneliness mother must have suffered in those long five years."[35]

In September, Edmund sent another $200 draft. "As I said before, do as you please about buying land and building on it. But as five acres is not sufficient for a farm you better enlarge it by buying next to what you have bought."[36]

On October 5, the streets were "thronged with men of every nation under heaven" when Edmund again wrote to Mary Ann. He explained that California wanted families to form a permanent, settled population.

This photograph of Mary Ann Booth was taken in the early 1850s when Edmund Booth was mining for gold in California. From the Booth family album, courtesy of The Haggin Museum, Stockton, California.

Were it not for the distance, deserts, Indians, this country would settle with farmers ten times as fast as Iowa. At least such is my fixed opinion. It (Calif.) is certainly in health climate alone worth twenty Iowas. Tell me if any of our neighbors are calculating on a removal next Spring. I would rather buy in Cal. Since it has become a State those who hold under Mexican grants are ready to sell to avoid taxation on so many square leagues of land. . . . If you were all here—Mother, Henry, Hannah, etc.—I should not feel the smallest inclination to return to Iowa.[37]

Mary Ann wrote to Edmund in October, "I thank God that you are still well." She was looking forward to moving into her own home and told him, "I shall be very happy to live in our own home as heaven. . . . I cannot be happy to live with Mr. Ford's folks who are still cruel to us, I have not time to write about them. When you come back I shall tell you what they have done to us badly. Hannah and Julia are hateful women."[38]

Julia had mocked Mary Ann's less-fortunate circumstances by saying that her father, Henry Booth, had more money than she did. Mary Ann had complained in August that Henry would not let her borrow $.50 even though she had $10 worth of gold dust and would pay him back. She perceived the mistreatment to be due, in part, to her deafness. She wrote in the margins of her October letter:

> Why they are cruel to me, because I am deaf. alike [sic] why the Masters are cruel to the slaves because they are black. . . . They always slight the deaf mutes because they think that the mutes know nothing about any thing in the world as Julia says. So they do not know how they hurt my feelings thousand times.[39]

She mentioned she had not seen Edmund's mother for about a month, and she did not want to see the Fords. Strangers, she said, seemed to treat her and the children better than relatives did. She told Edmund that Hannah or Gideon had opened a private letter from him without asking her first. Hannah appeared to be controlling, and in regard to this issue Edmund's mother may have been in agreement with Mary Ann. Edmund's mother mentioned to Mary Ann that she wanted to move back to Fairview from Anamosa, but Hannah was against it.

Shortly after they moved into their new house, Mary Ann began planning a rail fence around the 5 acres. She bought back their old cow for $15 and hired a man to cut 2½ tons of hay and haul and stack it. She hired Perkins, their deaf friend, to cut down the large patches of hazel brush and dig up hundreds of scrub oaks of all sizes. Without a brush scythe available, Perkins and Thomas had to use an axe. Thomas suggested a quicker way to clear the land, but his plan had near-tragic consequences.

> I finally persuaded [mother] to let me try setting fire to the brush and grass. Well, that was a success all right, and you can guess I was a terrified boy when the flames, seemingly caught by a fresh wind, swept southeasterly over

the premises and the hills and valleys south of the Military and the Wyoming road, all day long, clear down to the river bank and eastward for at least a mile, and it may have been much farther.[40]

Even though Mary Ann was deaf, she found great comfort in attending church. In 1851, a white frame church was built on the north side of Main Street for the members of the First Congregational Church (organized in 1846). This was the first frame church in the county. She also found greater comfort in her new home. She set up a cheese press in the front-yard, with a peck measure for the cheese mould, a heavy, 10-foot plank for a lever, and big rocks for exerting pressure. She and Thomas took care of the family cows and built a double-rail shed. Thomas was too frightened to set out after dark on the cow paths or timber roads to fetch water or retrieve the cows without his mother. While with his two cousins, he had a particularly frightening experience with a wildcat, which fortunately was scared off by their dogs.

Mary Ann wasn't afraid of wildcats or anything else. She never hesitated a moment to go with Thomas on a hunt for the cows on dark nights in the "Big Woods." As an adult, Thomas remembered that he "never saw a man or boy who would anymore dare go into the yard where [the cow] was kept with her calf than into a lion's cage. But mother was never afraid, and she was the only one who could milk her at such times . . . the cow seemed to have some sort of an intuition of mother's courage or perhaps a realization of her uniform kindness, and never harmed her."[41]

Mary Ann did need Thomas's ears at times, especially when picking blackberries among the yellow rattlesnakes.

Mother wanted me along no doubt because my ears were quick to detect the always startling, whizzing rattle of that dangerous reptile. She could not hear and was in constant peril of walking right on a coiled-up rattler all ready to strike the foot or ankle with its poison-filled fangs. That thrilling zing-g-g, once heard, can never be forgotten. In the woods or on the prairies it was the same—always dangerous—for the black rattlers of the prairies were equally venemous with the yellow variety.[42]

In her October letter Mary Ann reported that she now weighed 121 pounds, Thomas was 62 pounds, and Harriet 31. Harriet could use sign language skillfully with her mother, although she was only three years old. "She can talk by signs with me as well as any mutes." Mary Ann told Edmund that even though their daughter hardly knew him, she missed him. At one point, Harriet had been confused when another man had stopped by the house; she asked Mary Ann if the gentleman was her father.[43]

Mary Ann was an artist in curling Hattie's hair and preparing her children for the daguerreotype photographer. The picture of Hattie, with her rosy cheeks, must have thrilled her father, as did Mary Ann's soft smile, although he reported Thomas' countenance as "solemn as a tombstone."[44]

Mary Ann's brother George visited her for two weeks to assist her with the house and the fence around it. He brought 21 yards of carpet, a little parlor stove, and a piece of sheet iron to put under it. The beautiful carpet was large enough for several rooms. "It will make my room much warmer and more comfortable for the winter," Mary Ann wrote to Edmund. She gave George some money to buy a cooking stove, a table, a keg of mackerel, and other supplies in Dubuque. The new house would be finished by the end of October, and the family was planning to move in the next month.[45]

I shall bring our children up better. . . . Harriet is fat and healthy. Thomas is also. We have not had miniatures yet, for I have no money to go to Dubuque. I am alone in the garret while I am writing this but now Harriet just comes in and sees me writing. . . . she will begin to go school next spring. She will be four years old in June 17. I believe you remember it. She always talks about apples which you will send her by and by before she goes to bed every night ever since now. I laugh at her, because she keeps talking about apples and [which] you will . . . give her by and by.[46]

Mary Ann said that she and Thomas had seen Mr. Livermore again and were concerned about how the Fairview farm had been neglected.

Livermore wanted to purchase this land, but he had not fulfilled his responsibility in repairing the fences. Mary Ann was upset, and with Thomas's help, met with Harrison Joslin to split and haul the fence rails for $28.
Edmund encouraged her to have Thomas check on the progress of this
job. There is a possibility that with Edmund away from home, some people may have taken advantage of the deaf woman in their business dealings.

Edmund sent Thomas a $10 piece to get *Bancroft's History of the
United States,* which he highly recommended. He told Thomas that the
book was by far the best of the kind. Bancroft was yet alive and Edmund
knew him personally. He had been a schoolmaster in Northampton, Massachusetts, then Secretary of the Navy of the United States, and afterwards
minister to the Court of St. James (London). In December, Edmund
wrote:

> Doubtless you will wish to know how I kept Thanksgiving. It was Thanks-
> giving here on the same day as in all the other states, and I kept it, as most
> others did, by keeping at work. A man who comes to Cal. is very much like
> a sailor who goes on a three years' whaling voyage. He has no family, no
> relations around him. He must eat his Thanksgiving dinner with chance
> friends or alone.[47]

In this letter, Edmund again showed how he had to communicate daily
as a deaf man—through gestures and guesswork: "A short time after, I
was passing a Mexican unloading melons from a wagon. I pointed to one
that you would call of fair size, and asked the price. He held up two fingers. I asked . . . bits? He nodded. Thinking he misunderstood me or I
him, I pulled out a quarter. He shook his head. Then I said pesos . . .
dollars. He nodded."[48]

Watermelons, together with cucumbers, lettuce, muskmelons, green
corn, and other produce, were frequently available in the Sonora market,
fresh from the farms in San Francisco and other towns on the Bay. This
was the case the year round. Edmund saw a cabbage weighing 36 pounds
and asked his son what he thought of a potato 33 inches in circumference.
He told Thomas to measure his head and see.

On December 4 and 5 it rained hard; with the abundance of water and the sky clearing, Edmund made plans to go with a group of miners to Columbia. He wrote to Thomas, "I suppose you are now in winter weather, and attending school. Study well but not to excess—children are sometimes injured by excessive study."[49]

Later that week, Edmund sent Mary Ann a book about "Spirit Rappings," a way to communicate with loved ones in the afterlife. "I do not mean to say that I am a believer," he wrote, "but I cannot help thinking there is some truth in spiritual communication with the other world. Should these manifestations be actual truth and not trickery, or mere imagination (and I see no cause to suppose they are so) then our departed Harriet is often near and watching over us."[50]

He explained that in California, away from home and loved ones, idleness was an "intolerably tiresome kind of labor."

> One must read or seek amusement or dissipation or go to work or else go and hang himself, and this is no fancy. Except on Sundays or when it rains, I do not pass a single day in idleness, and keeping head and hands busy, time passes rapidly . . . . If I had not a relish for reading, I should be as wretched as are many others who, to relieve themselves, plunge into vice—A bull & bear fight comes off today—Such takes place almost every Sunday. I have visited none and never will—It is vulgar & brutish.[51]

Edmund was a caring and dedicated father. His passion for reading books and newspapers and remaining current with world events, despite his isolation in the West, emerges as a prominent feature in his correspondence throughout his stay there. This love for reading, too, is a quality he attempts numerous times to impart to his children through his letters. In December 1851, he mailed several letters to Mary Ann, but the weather was not favorable for a trip to Columbia. Thus, he found himself in "forced idleness." On one Sunday, the weather was warm and sunny, and he wrote that "nothing is so hard to do as to do nothing."[52] He marked his December 21 letter "Private" and mailed it to Mary Ann from Chili Camp. "I am sorry for your troubles," he told her, "but *patience*. I require and use more patience here than ever I did at home. I do believe that my coming to Cal. has been beneficial. I have now sent home over $500, and shall probably send more when I go to Sonora."[53]

He encouraged Mary Ann to cultivate her reading as well. He sent her a Texas newspaper containing a letter from Judge Barry of Sonora about the lack of fitness of many emigrants living in California. He mentioned that Barry was a friend of his, again showing that deafness posed no great barrier to him in his pursuit of communication with other intelligent men. Regarding her difficulties with Thomas, Edmund recommended channeling the young boy's energies into something constructive:

> He has much natural energy, and it works of course. It is the case with all strong and healthy children. You must have a garden by our house next spring and Thomas must plant and hoe and weed it. It will enable him to work his energies to good purpose. He will be learning to work, and will direct his mind and strength to something useful; and with you and Harriet, and perhaps with me also, will enjoy the fruits of his labor. A garden does not require constant labor except for a few days.[54]

In the same letter, Edmund told Mary Ann to "make your house as comfortable and pleasant as you can. It will have a great effect on the children. A pleasant home makes pleasant children. Make them love their home." He sent pictures and a map to the children to nail on the wall in one of the bedrooms in order to remember him. He told Thomas not to swear, and to listen to good men speak. He also insisted that Harriet must not go to school before she was five years old because "much mischief is often done to children by forcing the brain—and by confining them to one position on a bench all day. Their bones are growing and they need play and free action."[55]

"Home is heaven compared to the hard lonely life I lead here," he wrote a few days before Christmas. "No day ever passes but I think of you and the children and Mother several times *every hour*."[56]

Private

Private   Chili Camp Dec 21st 51

Dear Mary Ann
                                     This is for yourself
alone — not for others. I have just filled a
sheet for them in common with you; and now
I will have some private talk.

I was most sincerely glad to receive your
letters last evening I had been expecting them
but not till tomorrow, as I had not expected Buck
would go to Sonora. I am sorry for your troubles
but patience. I require and use more patience
here than ever I did at home. I do believe, that
my coming to Cal, has been beneficial. I have
now sent home over $500. and shall probably
send more when I go to Sonora. At present I do
not know when that will be, for I need rest on
Sundays, and I cannot well stop work on week
days. But certainly I will be in Sonora in two or
three or four weeks. I expect to do well here. My
partners were of my own choice (R specially)
and are good and intelligent men. When
we came here prospecting, B found a cousin
who has been of much service to us.

Do not let the follies of others (neighbors)
trouble your mind. It is only a crazy vanity on
their part that excites their ill humor. I never
heed such persons and I have seen many of them

Edmund spent nearly five years in California, but he corresponded regularly with his wife and children. Note the word "Private" at the top of this letter, dated December 21, 1851. Most of Edmund's letters were passed around to the whole family and, sometimes, to others in the community as well. This particular letter was for Mary Ann's eyes only. Courtesy of The Haggin Museum, Stockton, California.

SEVEN

Wearing Out

ఇశ్ర్యాశ్ర్య

EDMUND Booth stayed in California for another two years (1852–54). He missed his family greatly and craved news from home. After receiving a letter from Mary Ann in January 1852, he immediately wrote back, "We do not fully know the value of a home till we leave it. To live as I do, away from you all, away from home, in the hard, slavish, uncertain and varying life of a gold digger, requires a vast amount of resolution and fortitude. I do not like it, but I endure it for the sake of you and the children."[1]

He complained of the monotonous work of mining. Some days he made only $2. He had been doing "tolerably well" for some time, carting dirt to water and washing it, but he had spent about $100 in carting. All of the machines used by the miners needed a source of water. The long tom, a wooden trough 12- to 15-feet long, became one of the most commonly used machines. It included a metal bottom with a sieve to separate rocks and other objects from the dirt. Miners often formed partnerships because of the labor involved in working a claim. Edmund and his partners had created a sluice that was 500-feet long with a long tom at the tail, but they still were not able to work much without water.

All of Edmund's partners were from Boston. They had come together around Cape Horn by boat, arriving about the same time he reached California. All were married. One had four children, one three, and one had lost his only child. The group included Dr. Tarbox, a physician/surgeon/dentist, who had brought all his instruments with him. Tarbox was the son-in-law of John Dods, the author of the *Philosophy of Mesmerism*, which Edmund had sent Mary Ann the previous September. Edmund asked Tarbox to order a copy of another work by Dods, lectures on mesmerism

The "longtom" sluice functioned similarly to a rocker, but was much longer, often 10–15 feet. The miners shoveled dirt onto it and then poured water over the dirt. The heavier gold remained after the lighter dirt and gravel washed away. Reproduced by permission of the National Library of Australia.

delivered at Washington City at the request of members of the Cabinet and Congress. He had not given up hope that mesmerism could cure deafness. "You see," he added in his letter to Mary Ann, "I have as usual friends & associates among the well educated and intelligent—that is one great satisfaction, for ignorance is a very dull bore."[2]

Edmund was negotiating to purchase three good claims, a good wall-tent, table, furniture, provisions, long tom, and hose. These would cost him $400. His old long tom had drifted down stream and was never found. It had cost $33, but its replacement was only $9. When the rains came, he planned to run two toms and hire men to help him, paying each man $5 a day. "What we most want," he told Mary Ann, "is frequent showers of rain all winter and spring. I could make twenty dollars a day if we had rain." He predicted he would stay in California six or ten more months.[3]

In February 1852, Edmund received a letter from his son, Thomas, who expressed his desire to come to California: "If I once get there I don't

think that I would ever come back again if I got rich."⁴ Thomas then
described his daily routine to Edmund.

> I write a few lines then I go to my work and work a little while then I come
> in again. I go on in that way until I finish my letter then after my supper or
> any other meals I read untill I get sleepy then I go and lay on the lounge in
> a few [minutes] I fall asleep after I sleep awhile my mother awakes me then
> I go to bed I sleep all night when morning comes Mother calls me to make
> the fire I have not cut my feet or legs you need not be afraid that I will cut
> me if I get along this way all of my life it will be more than some people can
> do. I must finish my letter tonight because it must go away tomorrow morn-
> ing I must take them to the post office tonight I set here writing while
> Harriet is trying to make dolls out of paper and Mother is getting supper.
> There is no school now because that the scholars wont go but a few—so the
> school is broken up.⁵

LITTLE is known about what happened to Benjamin Clough, Edmund's deaf friend who accompanied him across the Plains. Edmund had
written to Mary Ann in March 1850 that he thought that Clough was still
in Weaverstown where they had gone their separate ways in the mines. But
Lewis Perkins told Mary Ann that Clough left California for Nevada in
1851. Edmund's sister Hannah had written that Clough sent her husband
money through a man traveling home to Iowa.

In her March 15, 1852, letter, Mary Ann commented that Clough had
been quite successful at gold mining, although in a separate letter written
on March 25 she indicated that this was not substantiated. In the March
15 letter she also demonstrates some practical good sense.

> I am jealous of Clough. I wish that it was you. If you had $20,000 like him
> you would be on your way for home now. I am very sorry that you can not
> get water enough to wash dirt out of gold dust. If we move there how can
> we get water enough to cook and wash our clothes? I often wish that a
> clairvoyant would tell you here gold is immense to take out [at] once. I
> believe that we shall better go to California than staying in Iowa which is
> good for nothing for us to live for.⁶

Later that year, May Ann learned that Clough lost his money gambling. Edmund responded to her on August 8, explaining that he had known many such cases. He never gambled himself, knowing that where one succeeds, ten lose. One of his partners lost $200 in a night—all he had.

Edmund's letters of January 21, 1852, arrived in Anamosa in mid-March. Mary Ann read hers and then let Mr. Skinner read the nonprivate one to others. In her response, she told Edmund she had grown a good crop of oats and planned to hire someone to harvest it soon—"I believe that I shall sell them to the merchants in this town, but I must wait, till one bushel will cost 20 or 25 cents, and now it costs 15 cents."[7] The busy deaf woman also sold oats to emigrants passing by the house on their way to California. She was unable to build the stable for the cattle that winter because there had been no lumber at the mills. The cattle had survived the winter and their old cow was expecting a calf very soon. Nor did she have a kitchen built yet, although she expected one soon. She also reported that Henry Booth had begun to build a large house about 20 or 30 rods from the house in which she and the children were living.

This is one of Mary Ann's most telling letters. In it she reveals not only her skills at handling the financial affairs at home, but also her ability to handle her husband from a distance of thousands of miles. She pulls at his heartstrings while simultaneously laying on guilt about his taking so long to find enough gold for them to live comfortably. As she watched groups of emigrants pass by her house every week, she contemplated making the trip to California. Her desire to be with Edmund and have her family whole again was tempered by her practicality—"I hardly think that I can leave my first comfortable home that I ever had and go to Cal. to live in a hut or worse house again, but I hated to live here for the coldest winter that I ever lived in Iowa." She was curious about whether certain fruits could be grown in California. She showed her own powers of observation and conjecture by noting that most of the emigrants passing by were carpenters and cabinet makers, leading her to wonder whether there would be enough lumber for building houses. "If you get one good house as mine," she told Edmund, "I shall be very glad to go there for health and climate. Thomas wishes very much that he can go there this spring, and thinks that he can get rich himself to dig gold."[8]

Mary Ann had another reason for offering to come to California—she wanted to have more children:

> My wish that you should be rich, for I wish that we shall be sure to live easy, and comfortably; therefore we shall be happier. I fear that you can hardly get rich [at] once, for it must keep you away from us and home so long. I do not like it. You say that there are plenty of gold on the surface of California. Why dont you get it and do try to get it luckily once and return home or send money us to go there for a permanent home to raise more children for I am tired to have only two children. I wish that I had six or ten children now. You know that I love children more than all gold. You will laugh at me about raising more children but I can not help it, for I love baby, as little girls love their dolls.[9]

ॐ१ॐ

PEOPLE continued to pour into California. One thousand Chinese immigrants had arrived in San Francisco at the end of March, and there were reports that 2000 more were on the way. "Three thousand Americans are on the Isthmus, and I suppose fifty thousand will cross the deserts this summer. In all, probably we shall have a hundred and fifty thousand added to the population of the State during the coming eight months. It is a madness. . . . It will cure itself by ruining thousands; but will at the same time settle the State with permanent families, and that is the chief good."[10] The rainy season ended in April, and Edmund joined a company of four men fully engaged in digging a 40-foot hole. He wrote to Mary Ann that he "may pocket ten thousand from it & may not one hundred. It is uncertain like all other places until we are near the bottom."[11] By late April, Edmund had dug 30 feet into the east bank of Wood's Creek. The stones lay so thickly together that every inch of the way had to be made with pickaxes. "We wash but little of it and that pays four or five dollars a day to the hand. Much that we dig pays nothing."[12] Their goal was to reach the old bedrock of the stream where it had run years before. This could not be done until June when the water in the hills had run off or dried so that it would not come into the hole faster than they could pump it out. Edmund felt that their claim was a good one, but he would not know until they had gone deeper. "It is large enough for a year's work—but I do not intend to stay so long. Still I will not go home until I get *enough*," he told Mary Ann. "You must have *patience* and *resolution* and *wait*."[13]

While Mary Ann and the children waited, Edmund suggested that Thomas write to him more often.

> Let him write in his own way. I can easily read and understand him and the ability of putting his thoughts to paper thus early is something. He will improve as he grows and practises. I hope he will cultivate the garden—He will learn something by it and especially that he is able to do something useful—I repeat that I will give him a dollar for his largest melon. Let him weigh it and tell me the weight.[14]

❧✦☙

IN EARLY May Mary Ann went into town with Thomas on business, not expecting a letter from Edmund, so she was excited to receive one. But the excitement soon turned to disappointment again. "Before we went out of the PO I was in a hurry in opening it, with hoping to hear some good news about getting much money and your coming back home, but I found nothing in it about your coming." The emigrants passing by to settle in Oregon and California were constant reminders of her husband being away for so long. "I saw many women and little children and ladies. They drove their ox teams with from five to seven yokes with each team and few horses and mule teams. They appeared respectable and rich folks. I confess that I almost cried to go with them too this spring."[15]

Edmund had sent her several books, including *Consuela* and the *Heir of West Wayland*, but Mary Ann complained, "I can never read these books again, for I have no time to read, for I must piece calico and quilt four [or] five quilts this summer—I have my old quilts worn out—and take care of my garden to keep weeding and cleaning." She planned to grow a nice garden the coming summer. "I hope that you shall be at home at that time to see our garden. Dont fail to come this year. If you dont come this year I must be given up and shall have no patience to wait for you longer. Thomas also feels impatient to wait for you longer. That he cannot go to

SAN FRANCISCO—FROM THE HILLS WEST.
PUBLISHED AT THE "NOISY CARRIER'S" PUBLISHING HALL.

San Francisco in 1852, from stationery used by Edmund Booth. Courtesy of The Haggin Museum, Stockton, California.

school much, for he must plant our garden first. School will commence tomorrow, Monday—a minister will teach."[16]

Ten-year-old Thomas was now in charge of cutting the firewood with an axe. The nearest well was beyond his Uncle Henry's house and the nearest after that was a half-mile distant. During the winter he had hauled his small wagon from Fawn Creek, a half-mile east, throughout the cold winter. The family did not have overcoats or overshoes, and the roads were often snow-covered and icy. Thomas planted the garden in May and then returned to school, where he did very well.

I was always among the first chosen on "spelling down" and "spelling across," and sometimes spellings schools were held in the country as well as in town. These matches were often very exciting, especially when different schools were pitted against each other. Then every day we were called out on the floor in a long string, and had to "toe the crack" in the floor, and as we were all or nearly all barefooted in the summer months, the array of toes was usually interesting, and sometime quite startling, as to shape, size, and cleanliness, or the lack of it. . . . This was great fun for the good spellers, and kept the class in a quiver of excitement, especially for the good spellers, while the poor ones dolefully maintained their accustomed position at the foot of the class. One term I had the best record for being at the head until next to the last day, when Maria Ford, my cousin, caught up and we were even. The last night I was at the head, and missed a word, and she spelled it, and went above me. This put me one behind, and the prize—a book— went to Maria. I went to my seat when the lesson was ended, put my head down on the desk, and proceeded to shed a gloomy assortment of briny tears.[17]

Thomas soon won a prize. For excelling in geography, he was given a book titled *The Life of Benjamin Franklin.*

ON MAY 25, Edmund described his prospects for the summer as "very good." He and two others in the company had taken out $34 in one day. Another day, they got $30, but then they had to wait a week to continue. He was now near Sonora, sinking a shaft into the claim he shared with five men. He decided that "if it does not pay well, I will sell it and go to Yankee Hill where the ground is higher and the air more cool."[18]

He moved around quite a bit—Chili Camp, Sonora, Wood's Creek, Yankee Hill. So did his friends. His partner at Yankee Hill, the lawyer, had a share in four different claims. He worked one and put hired men on the rest. He also owned a share in a claim with Edmund. The partners took care of each other's interests so they could work more than one claim at a time.

Edmund had not written to Mary Ann for several months, and this letter on May 25 indicated that he had clearly changed his mind about Mary Ann and the children coming to California.

I do not wish to remove you to this state now if ever. The climate is *good* but the people very unsettled. Land titles are all in doubt, and [there are] many other evils. I would prefer to wait and let order come out of chaos. A few years will make a great change in the appearance of things. The climate will bring many thousands of good people whom gold would not draw away from their old homes.[19]

He wrote of the fine moonlit evening and how he had just finished supper, which he cooked himself at a fire in back of the tents. "I was about to send you more flowers. I kept them a week and they faded and looked so dark and ugly that I threw them away and concluded not to send more."[20] He took joy in his surroundings despite the constant disappointments with the weather and bad luck.

> This afternoon we discovered the nest of a humming bird in our hole—The hole is about 30 feet square and perpendicular on the bank side where it is 12 or 14 ft. deep. Some roots project from near the top. On one of these— not as large as your little finger and shaded by other larger roots above which are covered with earth, the bird built its nest during our late absence. It is hatching and we shall not disturb it. While it left its nest for a half hour I pulled myself up by the large roots, sitting on the shoulder of a man and saw two little eggs of the size of the end of your little finger less than half an inch long. The nest is the size of a half hen's egg. The inside is not larger than mother's thimble.[21]

He described the vegetable and flower gardens and reflected, "I see flowers in large variety and by thousands every day, such as I never saw in the East." He also told Mary Ann about a possible problem with timber, which was plentiful on the mountains but not on the plains or prairies. He predicted that in a few years Californians would need to use coal for fuel or else bring wood in by railroad from the Sierra Nevada mountains.

He was indeed in a good mood while writing this letter, closing with, "Keep in good spirit, *all of you*. Let the world go as it will, be cheerful, active and good-hearted. It does much to preserve health and happiness. Goodbye and God bless you all."[22]

Edmund spent the Fourth of July in Columbia and then back to Yankee Hill. On Sunday morning, July 11, he came back to town to mail a letter. He had earned $130 from his claim, and he had ground enough for four months' work. He wrote to Mary Ann,

You express regret that I did not say in my letter of Feb. when I am coming home. I do not exactly know myself—but one thing I know and that is that I am doing *well*—making from $30 to $90 per week. Last night we divided the profits of the week's work (of five days, Monday, 5th, being the 4th of July). My share was $48.93 cts. We are three men in the Co. It has paid as high as $90 a day—about ten days ago. [23]

Edmund thanked Mary Ann for the mandrake pills she had sent. He also described at length his recent bout of illness.

Without them I could have little hope of curing any serious disease by which I might be attacked. I have again very recently proved their efficiency, having had a severe fit of sickness, having as a foundation a cold which I had entirely neglected for two months. One night when the day's work was over, I found myself out of health—Next day went to Sonora—grew worse—stayed there—obtained emetic, salts and senna, of a physician, or rather he administered them, as he lived in the same house and was an old acquaintance. Eat nothing for three days—and finally gave a Dutchman a dollar to go and bring my carpet bag from up Wood's Creek 1/2 mile, where I had left it in the house of some friends. From this I took six and next day seven Mandrake pills and the tide turned—I had become so weak as hardly to be able to walk but from this time mended rapidly and lo and behold! it came out that I had the *SMALL POX*!

This disease has prevailed for two months in and around Sonora, but I believe not over 20 or 30 persons have had it—Four have died of it. One of my late partners on Wood's Creek has it now very badly.[24]

The nine days' idleness due to his illness cost him nearly $100 for board, medicine, and the men he hired to work on his claim at $5 per day. Once again, he told Mary Ann that "the time of going home will depend much on the water I have here. I do expect to go next winter." In the meantime, he suggested, Mary Ann should decide about selling some cattle and their town lots in Fairview: "I leave you to fix the price but certainly they are worth more than fifty dollars."[25]

On August 8, Edmund was still in Columbia, living in a pine log house 10 × 12 feet, 5 logs high, with a double canvas roof that kept out the sun's heat in summer and the rain in winter. Despite its size, he had a fireplace and chimney. It was his own house, given to him in payment of a debt by his late partner, who had killed himself. He looked forward to being "at home in the new house in a nice warm parlour next winter," he wrote, but he was uncertain "about the time I return and you are right to put in a good stock of patience and wait calmly." He assured Mary Ann that the smallpox was completely gone and he expected to come home with "the same handsome [face] I brought away."[26] He admitted that he wrote very long letters, but he explained to Mary Ann that "in thinking of home I think ten thousand things; and wish to ask ten thousand questions and make ten thousand remarks, as most men would every day if they had breath and brains, however shallow, talk the thousand cartwads of nonsense."[27]

His pine log cabin had a canvas curtain door 4-feet high, through which his 6-foot-3-inch frame dodged in and out head first. The door was inadequate for keeping animals out, however. One day, an ox looking for salt pushed through the canvas door and devoured all of Edmund's potatoes, onions, and bread, as well as knocking over and scattering everything else.

At the end of August, Edmund was once again bored with waiting for the rain to come. "I assure you it is hard work to be idle, whatever indolent people may say," he complained. "Yesterday I slept through nearly the whole afternoon and as a consequence read (being unable to sleep) till daylight this morning and was up before the sun." He told Mary Ann he wished he was good at etching so that he might send his family pictures of the wild and rough scenery of the various places where he had worked.[28]

☙❧

ON NOVEMBER 9, 1852, Mary Ann wrote to Edmund from Dubuque, Iowa. She explained that her sister and brother-in-law, Emily and George Fifield, thought it unfair for her to stay at home with the children and keep house "without any man to help me this cold winter to get my wood and provisions." So she decided to go live with them. She would help Emily with the household tasks and Thomas would assist with chores. "If you are coming back this time," she told Edmund, "we shall return home immediately."[29]

Mary Ann was pleased that Emily's husband had learned to talk with her "with his fingers." She hoped that Thomas would converse with his aunt and uncle and that they could help correct his "rough manners." Mary Ann's brother Harrison was also a fine and intelligent man, and she hoped that he would teach Thomas in his office sometimes so she would not have to pay for schooling. She urged Edmund

> to be careful not to tell anybody that you are going to start for home with so much money with you, for I am afraid that they may be cunning to follow and kill you on the way and rob your money. . . . I never tell any body about your money, for I am in danger if I live in my house alone, with so many dollars in the drawers. I should be murdered and robbed.[30]

She planned to let the farm rent free for a year, if the renter would split new rails and repair the fence. She was offered $30 in trade for three lots in Fairview, but she refused the offer based on Edmund's advice that the lots were worth $50. However, she could not sell the lots without Edmund's signature. "You must be careful not to overwork so hard," she wrote. "I hope that I shall see you soon and [you will] live with us in our new house comfortably and I shall not part with you again. . . . I hope that God will take care of you while you are on the way for home." She then asked, "If you do not come home, what shall I do with our farm?"[31]

THE new year arrived with Edmund still in California. He wrote from Columbia on January 8, 1853, to let his family know that he was all right despite the scarcity and high price of provisions in the mines. "I am in no danger of starving . . . [if only that] provisions are to be had at some price," he explained. "I have enough for a week to come and my claim pays well when the sky will let us work." The past week he and three partners had taken out $76. His board cost him $8–10 a week. He could not get bread or any meat at any price.[32]

On January 10, he warned her not to "suppose, as your letter indicated, that I am growing rich. Very few do that here. Perhaps one in a thousand. Still I am doing very well, or rather I should be doing well if the rain would but cease and let us work more than one or two days in the week." He was pleased that she and the children were with Emily. He encouraged them to stay if they were enjoying the visit and suggested that Thomas might be able to attend a better school in Dubuque than the one in Anamosa.[33]

Mary Ann's March letter mentioned an uneducated deaf man named John Healey from Dubuque who had emigrated to California with his family. Healey had returned and met with Lewis Perkins in Anamosa and explained that he planned to take his family back to California to both farm and dig for gold. Mary Ann doubted that this was wise, since Healey had neither yet staked a claim, nor bought a farm and the gold rush had already attracted too many people. Mary Ann tried once again to pressure Edmund to return. She told him she was worried about her own health. "Sometimes my heart is painful. If you do not come back sooner I expect that I shall sometimes die suddenly. I do not know what will our children do. . . . I wish that you would go and see a clairvoyant . . . and tell him to go and examine my heart and ears which always itch and often become very sore."[34]

Edmund responded by sending home money. He told Mary Ann to "pay all debts and get the land near the house at Anamosa broken, so that it will be ready to cultivate next spring—I shall be at home next winter to prepare the fence." Pleading for her patience, he wrote, "my expectations of last winter failed but I am doing well now—You are happier than I am, as you have the children with you and I am alone. Keep your head or hands or both busy—Work or read as you please, and time will not appear so long."[35]

Despite his optimism, Edmund was discouraged. Back home, William Haddock had begun publishing the *Anamosa News and Journal*, a weekly newspaper. New businesses were opening and Anamosa was growing. But in California, Edmund could hardly find enough to eat. The shortage of food was not helped by the fact that his ox devoured his provisions three more times before he had fixed the door.

Staying away from his family for so long, now more than three years, became more and more of a struggle. He described it as being "almost death," and asked Mary Ann to send him the Anamosa paper frequently.[36]

because they are vulgar, as I have seen them much while you are absent from home. pray do come back, do try to come come, come along. I hope that God will make your return home in safety and join me again. God bless you. farewell.
M. A.

Anamosa March 13 /53

My dearest husband

I resume my dear pen with pleasure and I am sorry that I did not answer your two letters dated 8 and 10 of January immediately. I received them on the third of this month. I expected to answer them last Sunday, but I was interrupted by my brother Harrison who came and staid till Monday. he came to attend some business for Geo and Clark and returned home the same day, Monday. He said that Mr Fifield's family is all well and is expecting to go East this Spring, for his father has been sick and is not expected to live and wanted to see his son, but Emily did not conclude to go with him, for her baby will be in danger of travelling and exposing to the cold and wet weather. If Mr Fifield expects that he will return Dubuque next summer Emily will remain here or in Dubuque. I wrote and requested her to come and remain with us untill he return. I expect to hear from them soon, I shall know more about which Emily will remain or not.

When I received your last letters, I became sad that provisions are high and I fear that you can never return home. I felt painful that you did not say anything about your coming back in your last letter. I hope that provisions go low price now and that you have not been starving before.

Were you ever starving before? I hope that you will answer. no.

A page from the March 19, 1853, letter written by Mary Ann Booth to Edmund Booth. Mary Ann's letters were filled with news about Thomas and Hattie, friends and relatives in Anamosa, and her desire to have a home of her own. Courtesy of The Haggin Museum, Stockton, California.

Edmund had recently read *Uncle Tom's Cabin* and was glad that Mary Ann and Thomas had a copy. "I have been in the South and know that it is not a whit exaggerated," he told them.[37] A week later, he wrote to Thomas,

> Tomorrow, I send you a Chinese book, and also another book entitled "Crayon Sketches" of men who have *made themselves*, who are distinguished as public speakers and writers; and who mostly speak and write for the present and the future, not, as do most of our politicians, for the past. The work is racy and life like—Among the characters [included], you will find Horace Greeley, whose paper, the New York Tribune, will probably reach you with this or soon after. It appears that the money [$4 for two years' subscription] I sent for it last Autumn was lost. I will send again for it tomorrow.
>
> I hope you will read that paper habitually; not merely the news, but also the *reviews of books, sketches* [and] *lectures*, etc. It is important that you should acquire a knowledge not only of words and ability to use them, but also of ideas—a large range of facts and ideas. These are to be learned not all in a day or in a year, but as a bee gathers honey, little by little. . . . Do not suffer the loss of the "Sketches." It will bear more than one reading, and the men described in the work are, with one or two exceptions, living men in middle life. The lady (Mrs. Harriet Beecher Stowe), who wrote "Uncle Tom's Cabin," is a sister to the two Beechers of the "Sketches." Genius, united with Conscientiousness and Humanity, runs in that family.[38]

On July 22, Mary Ann wrote a touching letter to Edmund, which began, "My dear husband. . . . Last Tuesday morning I received your interesting letter of June 12. I quickly sat down to open and read it and most cried, for I overjoyed to hear that you said that you would be at home next winter. . . . I wish that you will start for home early in the fall and be home before Christmas or New Year's, so I may make you feast here."[39]

She told him that the field was looking good with rich crops and that he would have a nice farm upon his return. Harrison Joslin had found timber, and split and hauled 745 rails to Mary Ann's farm. All this cost $18.62, which she paid him. Around the same time she bought some provisions for the summer.

My money about twenty dollars are left in my own pocket. I must be careful to save these money to buy hay for our young two cattle for next winter. Here one ton of hay sells at two dollars and also buy some lumber more for our kitchen (for siding and lathing). I think best that you will not send me any more because you will be at home soon.

Behold my writing looks very bad, because my pen is dull. I wish you will buy a real golden pen when you are on your way home, so it will be kept good for many years. I hope that you will wear better dresses when you return home. You must throw your mining dresses away! or sell them to the miners.[40]

Thomas was doing a good job with the garden, and when he rested, he read the newspapers his father sent regularly. The family enjoyed the *New York Tribune*. Emily's husband was thinking of buying Mr. Woods' newspaper in Dubuque, but he was waiting for George H. Walworth to return home to help with the costs. "I have justly ate supper and washed my dishes," Mary Ann wrote, "and took my pen again to finish this tonight . . . Our children send their love to you." She added at the end of her letter, "Do not fail to return home early in the winter. I shall look for you in the stage which is passing and repassing by our house daily."[41]

In the fall of 1853, Edmund was working at Camp Seco and "Murphy's Diggings." In September he indicated that he was coming home in February, and asked Mary Ann send him more Mandrake pills for the trip. "I would like to be at home on Christmas and New Years day, but must defer. There is no employment so uncertain as gold mining," he told her, "and none that had so many drawbacks—and yet the very nature of the life and employment makes the miners a light hearted set of fellows when not at work."[42]

He had a scare when he received a letter from Mary Ann in someone else's handwriting. Mary Ann had taken ill and her brother Harrison had written about the fever and chills, attempting to convince Edmund to come home. Fearing the worst, Edmund took the letter into an adjoining saloon and read it as calmly as he could.

He wrote to Mary Ann on November 13, telling her that the news of her illness "came on me with a shock and I feel very sad." He said he would sell his investments "at any price" and leave on a steamer on December 1. He told Mary Ann that he had not made what he wished or expected, but he had done the best he could and he hoped she would be satisfied.[43]

Although Mary Ann recovered from the fever and ague without complications, she did not recover from her impatience with Edmund, who did not leave California on December 1, as he had promised. His decision to return home was likely influenced by a letter, now lost, that he received from Mary Ann some time in January or February 1854. This letter coupled with his own realization that he had spent five years with no great success, convinced him the time had arrived to give up. Even though he was working at Camp Seco with a young deaf partner, Herbert Weyhl, taking out $10 to $30 each day, Edmund knew it was imperative to return home.

Years later, Edmund remembered that Mary Ann's letter "was very urgent, and I concluded to return and no further delay."[44]

EIGHT

Home Again

❧❀❧

EDMUND Booth finally started for home some time in February 1854. He traveled to San Francisco by stage, waited with friends a few days until a steamer sailed, and then spent twelve days at sea. The California and Oregon Trails were still largely one-way routes westward, so the most popular and quickest way home was through Nicaragua and across the Gulf of Mexico. With about 500 other passengers, Edmund took a steamer to the foot of Lake Nicaragua, transferred on to one sternwheeler, and then another, which entered the San Juan River. He journeyed by mule across land to the Caribbean, taking note of the tropical vegetation and many curiosities on the way. After reaching the fort on the Caribbean side of Nicaragua Edmund boarded a large boat, but a gale at the western extremity of Cuba delayed his departure. After the storm abated, the ship turned northwestward and headed for the mouth of the Mississippi. His destination yet a long way off, Edmund went to his bunk.

During this voyage home Edmund read many newspaper reports about the growing strife between the North and South. His displeasure with slavery was so intense that he could never hold back his anger: "I told a couple of southern men of my California acquaintance that if the south wished to go out of the Union, to go and be hanged. They laughed but showed no anger. Told them I was tired of this strife and constant threats and complaints."[1]

As in California, people on the ship readily made acquaintances. "Good nature prevailed," he wrote; "we were all *going home*." Upon reaching New Orleans, the crowds scattered, those bound north walked along the long line of river steamers and consulted newspaper advertisements for dates of departure for St. Louis. Edmund found a boat scheduled to leave at 2:00 in the afternoon, and he paid $20 for a stateroom, board, and passage. There were repeated delays over the next three days, which Edmund surmised were caused by the desire "to procure more passengers and freight." Finally, on the fourth day, "the boat drew out and started up stream."[2]

The trip was a pleasant one until the boat ran aground below St. Louis, because it was too heavily loaded. A passenger boat following a mile behind was signaled, came alongside, and took off some passengers at $4 a head. Edmund was one of those passengers.

> I went with them for there was no knowing when the water would rise or the boat be got off by lightening cargo. I reached St. Louis, and here I wished I had stayed in California another month. The river above was closed by ice and only one steamer was advertised to try to break through the next day for Davenport, Iowa. It was in the closing days of February. I took passage on that one steamer. It was easy enough for the first few miles. After that it was rushing the boat and cutting away some rods, backing out and rushing in again, until about three or four miles below Keokuk, Iowa. There the contest was given up and we came to land. A dozen of us went ashore, kindled a fire for comfort while two men went inland on the hunt for a team to take the party forward to town. This came after some time and we all packed into the two horse wagon and reached Keokuk and the hotel in the course of the night. Next day took conveyance to Burlington and thence by stagecoach for Iowa City. . . . Next morning I took stage for Anamosa via Cedar Rapids, then a small straggling village. . . . this time sat outside with the driver, wishing to get a good view of the country while approaching home.[3]

In March 1854 there was not a mile of railroad or a telegraph line in the state of Iowa at the time. The Booth family had been anticipating Edmund's arrival, but they had no way of knowing exactly when he would be home. They knew it was a slow journey from California, and the last leg would be on Frink and Walker's four-horse coach line from Iowa City. Thomas, now twelve years old, kept watch on a log near the family's woodpile in front of the house. He gazed westward down the military road, and every now and then his heart would beat with excitement when someone came in sight. Late one afternoon he saw the figure of a large man approaching.

But finally, away down the street, perhaps a quarter of a mile distant, I saw a traveler approaching. As he came nearer I observed that he was carrying a carpet sack in one hand. He had on a light-colored but heavy overcoat and wore a new glazed cap. Surely it wasn't anybody I was acquainted with in this locality. This intensified my curiosity, and when the big man came straight toward me, put out his hand and exclaimed, "Home at last," I knew it was father! I verily believe I was the happiest boy in America at that moment.[4]

After greeting Thomas, Edmund quickly turned to the house with his son tagging close behind. As they rounded the corner of the house, Mary Ann flew out the back door, throwing her arms around her husband and kissed him. Hattie, who was only a year old when her father left for California, was now almost six and quite frazzled by her mother's behavior with the stranger who had just approached. "Naturally I was properly shocked," she wrote later, "and even the information it was father failed to satisfy me entirely that such conduct was proper."[5] Thomas described his father's arrival in more detail:

Father sat right down in the kitchen and fingers were flying in an instant. . . . After feasting my eyes on father's and mother's happy faces for a brief time, I was siezed [sic] with the natural impulse to run over and tell "gramma" that father had come home. Of course she and uncle Henry and Julia were greatly pleased—overjoyed, in fact . . . Father . . . did not delay too long in going over to see his mother and the rest.[6]

It was fortunate that Edmund did not prolong his stay further in California. His mother died of apoplexy on June 28, only a few months after he returned home. He was thus able to spend time with her before she passed away.

IT IS difficult to estimate Edmund's profits beyond expenses from the gold mining. He told his children more than once that he did "better than average." Throughout his stay in California he had sent Mary Ann drafts as well as some gold dust, nuggets, and coins. One evening soon after Edmund's return, Hattie found her parents sitting at a table, staring at two piles of $20 gold pieces. "I thought we were millionaires and was quite incredulous when both asserted it was not much." Thomas remembered seeing his mother ask his father directly how much he had brought home and, knowing that the children were looking on, he had responded, "Enough to be comfortable." His best discovery was a gold nugget worth $300, but, as Thomas later wrote, "every miner had a partner, perhaps two, and I have often thought that father, strictly honest himself and unusually unsuspicious, may have been cheated by dishonest partners—no telling how often or to what extent."[7]

Within a few days after his arrival Edmund bought 80 acres of wild prairie 3 miles north of Anamosa from his brother Henry. The price was $800, paid in gold. Edmund also gave Henry $300 for taking care of his family the first year he was in California. He bought a yoke of young white oxen for $75 and a second-hand wagon without a box for $25.

Despite the fact that he had not become wealthy, Edmund was nevertheless satisfied that he had left Hartford. A few months after his return, he received a visit by Samuel Porter, a teacher and editor of the *American Annals of the Deaf and Dumb*. During their discussion of Edmund's earlier dispute over salaries at the American Asylum, Porter told him that "the Board had found its mistake and had raised the salaries of deaf teachers to $400 for first year."[8]

Anamosa had prospered while Edmund was in California. The town now had a drug store, a dry goods store, and the "Boots, Shoes & Groceries" shop. Two miles west of town a steam mill sat in a deep ravine. Farmers driving their hogs to the river markets of Dubuque and Muscatine, the main trading centers of the day, would stop at the mill en route. The other businesses in town included brickyards, hotels, churches, blacksmith shops, grocery stores, printing offices, and tailor shops. At least a half-dozen physicians offered their services.

As the summer and fall passed, Edmund worked hard at re-establishing his homestead and supporting his family through farming. Slowly, the family grew accustomed to being together again. More than the children had to adjust to the burly deaf man at the Booth homestead. Thomas remembered that "the steers, no doubt frightened by father's strange voice, ran away the first thing they did. No damage, and they soon found out that father was the kindest owner and driver they ever knew, before or after."[9]

Thomas often helped his father on the farm. Together, they built a rail fence for the first 10 acres of the new property. Thomas was in awe of his father's strength and abilities.

> Father was 44, nearly, right out of the mines and with muscles of iron. He provided himself with axe, maul and iron wedges and at once went to work felling trees and splitting rails in the timber. I went with him and the team in the course of a couple of weeks and was astonished at the number of trees he had cut down and worked into rails—a dozen big piles, perhaps more. Of course they had to be hauled five miles to the farm.[10]

When he wasn't helping his father, Thomas joined his friends for hours on end under the Metcalf grist mill, fishing for rock bass and black bass. On one occasion a big catfish seized the hook, dragging Thomas into the deep, swift currents that swept under the mill. Fortunately he escaped tragedy and still managed to pull in the fish, marching home in triumph. The adventure did not scare him much. He returned many times again to enjoy listening to the droning hum of the mill's powerful water wheels, the moving belts, and large stones that transformed grist into flour to provide bread to people around the region.

Although Edmund had many rich experiences during the nearly five years he was a forty-niner, he missed seeing his children growing. Mary Ann had established a strong presence in family affairs and Edmund had to adjust to this as the Booth household settled into a routine again. Mary Ann had learned to operate the spinning wheel from her mother, and she deftly spun yarn for hours on end with a rhythm that charmed her children. She was also graceful at "jumping the rope." Thomas and his cousin

Julia enjoyed watching the deaf woman "dance" with an unequalled agility.

With these joys, however, also came the varied dangers of farming in the wilderness. Thomas particularly remembered two encounters with rattlesnakes, a danger to which his deaf parents were especially vulnerable.

> When mowing alone with a common scythe somewhere in the neighborhood of the Cass farm in 1854–5, [father] was startled at seeing a snake writhing and twisting just in front of him. An investigation revealed the amazing fact that he had decapitated a rattlesnake, that undoubtedly was coiled up, sounding his unheard warning, and would have struck father a death-blow if the sharp scythe had not caught his uplifted head. Think what would have been his fate a mile or more from any farm-house and three miles from home! It was certainly a providential escape, for which I feel he was very grateful.[11]

The other incident occurred inside their house. Thomas and Hattie slept in a trundle bed in the south bedroom. One morning when they awoke, they heard a strange, strident noise, which sounded like a rattlesnake. Thomas did not think it was possible, but that strange hiss prodded him to look under the bed. The snake had squeezed through a mouse hole in the corner of the bedroom. Thomas was able to dispatch it safely, leaving him to wonder what would have happened if the snake had found its way into his deaf parents' room.

EDMUND thrilled Thomas with his knowledge and experiences while they worked on the farm together or took walks in the woods. Edmund's love for poetry led him to recite long passages to his children by memory, enrapturing them with his knowledge of literature and instilling in them a love for Shakespeare, Scott, Byron, and other poets. He habitually stayed up until the early morning hours devouring poetry. Thomas recalled "sitting on his lap before the big fireplace while his words were as sweet music to my enraptured senses."[12]

In the fall and winter of 1854, Edmund cut fence posts for a neighbor's farm, and with hundreds of other men prepared rails for the Dubuque

Southwestern Railroad.[13] He bought a cross-cut saw, which he and Thomas used to cut large 8-foot-long white oak logs. They then hewed the logs on two sides and sold them for $.40 a tie. At noon, the men would gather around to eat their lunch and listen to Edmund expound on a public theme, historical fact, or a personal reminiscence. The clarity of his speech was not as important as the substance of his messages. One night when Edmund and Thomas were walking together along the road-side, just opposite the Gillen House on the corner of Main and Garnaville Streets, a pair of runaway horses nearly trampled them in the dark. Thomas heard the rush of hoof beats and resounding clatter and pulled his father toward the fence in the nick of time.

The money Edmund brought home from California did not last long. By the time winter came,

> Money was a mighty scarce article, but father made a deal with Secrest and I was happy. The deal was this: A load of long wood, 50 cents; for a pair of skates, 50 cents. Father was always indulgent, the oxen were hitched up the next morning and away we went two miles to the timber. It took all day for the trip. Then of course the skates had to be equipped with straps. Deal No. 2 was in order. Another day and another load of long wood for John Belknap fixed that all right. It was literally a 50-50 proposition successfully and joyously consummated. Two days, eight miles travel, toilsome labor for a man, boy and weary oxen, that doubtless wondered what it was all about—for a single pair of pot-metal muley skates—cost, $1.00.[14]

That winter, Thomas also took on his first paying job—kindling fires for six months at the schoolhouse at a salary of $.50 per month. By 9:00 each morning he was expected to have the large barn-size building warm for classes. The $3 he earned in six months paid for his own education. Hattie was attending school also, but the teacher never asked Edmund for another $3. Perhaps she did not press for the money out of appreciation for Thomas's work.

In the spring of 1855, Edmund and Thomas harvested about 150 bushels of wheat on the 10 acres they had fenced in the previous spring. They also broke 10 more acres for future crops. On July 27, 1855, Mary

Ann gave birth to a second son. Like his brother and sister, Frank Walworth Booth could hear. Thomas and Hattie had to adjust to the "changed situation resulting from the arrival of this squirming and sometimes slightly vociferous novelty."[15] Thomas remembered the smile on Mary Ann's face as she looked upon her new child.

ANAMOSA had two weekly newspapers—the *Anamosa News and Jones County Advocate* and the *Anamosa News & Journal*. These newspapers served the community until July 1856, when John E. Lovejoy founded the *Eureka*. Lovejoy was the brother of antislavery agitator Elijah Lovejoy and Owen Lovejoy, a distinguished orator who was elected to the House of Representatives that year. Elijah had been murdered by a proslavery mob in Alton, Illinois, in 1837; as a result Owen had become an even fierier abolitionist. John Lovejoy's views likely attracted Edmund to the newspaper. The Lovejoys and Walworths, Mary Ann's brothers in particular, were also long-time friends.

By 1856, debates over slavery were raging throughout the country. Abolitionists and proslavery forces openly advocated violence and several abolitionists were murdered in Kansas. The first issue of the *Eureka* came off the press in August 1856 as a weekly broadsheet carrying news, editorial comments, and advertisements. John Lovejoy invited Edmund to contribute an article to the new paper, and this proved to be a turning point in Edmund's life. His first article was published as the leading editorial. Charles L. D. Crockwell, a local druggist, took over the *Eureka* at the end of 1856. He continued to employ Edmund to write for the paper, and within a short time, Edmund was managing its publication as well. The paper had about 400 subscribers at the time.

The first *Eureka* office was in a little one-story brick building owned by John Green, a lawyer. It measured 12 × 16 feet and housed the printing press and all the necessary supplies. A few weeks after opening, Lovejoy moved to the second floor of a brick building opposite Mr. Green's, while waiting for Green's building to be finished. Green died before it was completed.[16]

Meanwhile, Thomas had completed what schooling was available in

Iowa, so Edmund and Mary Ann decided to send him to Kimball Union Academy in Meriden, New Hampshire. The school, which opened in 1813, prepared young men for the ministry. Mary Ann's brother, Clark, who lived in Boston and worked with his oldest brother James at the Walworth Manufacturing Company paid for Thomas's school expenses at the Kimball Union Academy. After spending 20 months at the Kimball Union Academy, Thomas returned home to help his father in the printing business. For about a year he was primarily the "roller boy" on the new Washington handpress.

In 1858, Edmund bought a half share of the newspaper from Matthew Parrott. The May 3, 1858, issue carried his name on the masthead. The *Eureka* provided Edmund with the opportunity to pursue a career that would use his intellect. His talents as a writer and newspaper editor blossomed quickly. He combined local news, his literary interests, and his expanding political views to produce a well-rounded, strongly Republican, newspaper. With his earnings from the gold mines long gone, he had to borrow $500 and mortgage his farm to pursue this new venture. Over the next five years, he was unable to pay his debts and the farm went under foreclosure for less than he had paid for it. Despite the financial losses, he loved the newspaper work and never considered returning to farming.

In January 1859, Crockwell left the newspaper business and Parrott and Booth renamed it the *Anamosa Eureka*. Crockwell's parting comment in the newspaper was that "we can assure the Republicans of Jones County that in Messrs Booth & Parrott they will find a team that, if WELL FED, will give a 'long pull, a strong pull and a pull altogether' for the cause of Human Rights."[17] Edmund Booth had found his life's work and pursued it with a passion.

As time went on, the *Anamosa Eureka* printing office continued to take on jobs of every kind. One of its advertisements offered to print catalogs, tickets, labels, cards, handbills, ball tickets, pamphlets, envelopes, programs, bullheads, bank checks, auction bills, blank notes, and show bills of fare. Edmund was never happier than when he was working the power press until the midnight hour. Through these years, he continued to gather small groups of friends, neighbors, his sons, even strangers, at the

THE ANAMOSA EUREKA.

TERMS—$2.00 A YEAR. INDEPENDENT IN EVERYTHING. (IN ADVANCE.)

VOL. XII. ANAMOSA, JONES COUNTY, IOWA, MAY 21, 1868. NO. 33.

Edmund Booth became part owner of the *Anamosa Eureka* in 1858, and sole owner in 1862. He took over editorial control of the paper on May 3, 1858. He and his son, Thomas Eyre Booth, together edited the newspaper for over 50 years. Photograph courtesy of The Haggin Museum, Stockton, California.

Eureka printing office to discuss topics related to history, good habits, or his ideals of life. He would talk about anything except gossip, which he detested. He was very generous in his business dealings and would even accept goods in lieu of cash payments for subscriptions to the paper or for printing jobs. In one note to subscribers, he wrote,

> We will take, in payment of subscriptions to THE EUREKA, wheat, corn, pork, beef, lard, and, in short, any kind of produce that we can eat or sell. Many persons in the county are owing us, and few are able to obtain much of the article called cash, at the present time. When such person or their neighbors are about coming to town, just deposit in the wagon the necessary amount of whatever it may be, and we will take it at regular prices and give a receipt therefore. This plan will accommodate those who desire our paper but are kept back from taking it by the difficulty of procuring money, and will also enable those who use, to liquidate. By doing as above, we shall be satisfied; subscribers will be satisfied; the merchants to whom we can sell what we cannot use, and who will in turn, sell us what we can use, will be satisfied, and there will be satisfaction all around. Is not this plan the most satisfactory that could be devised for the hard times?[18]

From the very beginning of his newspaper work, Edmund addressed the most sensitive national issues. He focused much of his energy on the abolition of slavery. Two days after James Buchanan's inauguration in 1857, the Supreme Court issued its ruling on the Dred Scott Case. This ruling held that blacks, whether slave or free, were not citizens of the United States; therefore, slavery could not be prohibited in the western territories. Like other abolitionists who had come to Iowa from New England and Ohio, Edmund was devoted to the opposition of slavery and support for the Union. As the agitation over slavery grew, his own Republican views strengthened. He wrote that the troubles of Kansas had brought to that territory a greater proportion of moral and intelligent men than is usually found. He advised others to look at Kansas and take courage. In an article titled, "Enslaving the Free Blacks," he wrote,

> The Cuba project, the Mexican seizure, the outrageously ridiculous Dred Scott decision, the Fugitive Slave Law, the attempted imposition of slavery

on Kansas, and the reducing of free black men and women to bondage, are all points which men are compelled to see whether they will or not, and which show, as clear as day, that the system they are designed to aid is a system of hell and the master thereof is the Devil.[19]

On New Year's Day, 1858, Edmund printed one of his poems in the *Eureka.*[20] His prescient poem comes from the soul, touching eloquently on what was to unfold in our nation over the next eight years. The composition of this patriotic verse was unsettling to proslavery supporters. Prophetic and powerful in its message, it is one of many examples of Edmund Booth's strong antislavery sentiments.

Carrier's Address

There is need
That some should suffer the extreme of wrong,
To waken him on hearts and rouse the strong;
Life without freedom is not worth its cost,
And freedom gone our very life is lost.
And what is left, aye, what is left?
Behold the vanished nations. 'Tis a story old.

Oh, thou fair land of Kansas, it is thine
To show that man is God-like still, Divine,
That he must struggle and advance, not fail,
That Right must ever, in the end, prevail,
That Error, Wrong and Tyranny shall fall,
That Beneficence shall rule over all,
That such is man's destiny and his right,
Else were the world one sad, eternal blight;
Press onward, therefore, men of heart and mind,
Press onward all, ye lovers of mankind,
Ye in whose bosom burns the soul that tells
Of Truth that pierces through a thousand hells,
And scatters fiends and firebrands from its path,
All heedless of their presence or their wrath.
As heedless now advance and aid the free,

And make of Kansas a Thermopylae.
'Tis she may save this nation from its grave,
And therefore tyrants shout she shall be slave,
Send back the bold defiance; shout it back,
And arm, if need be, for the warrior's track.

. . .

Let serviles base to oligarchies palter,
And bow and bend the knee, they have their pay;
For us 'tis death or freedom, come what may—
Come bloodshed and destruction, horrors dire,
Come all and drive us through the cleansing fire;
That fire shall melt our chain, where'er it sways,
And Freedom's glad sun shine on all the coming days.

Edmund was outspoken on other issues as well, including the national banking system and the women's rights movement. His years in California gave him the wisdom that only experience can provide, and he often shared his personal views in his editorials. When a report came out about the discovery of more gold in California in June 1859, five years after his return to Iowa, he published the following note in the *Eureka*:

Our experience of nearly five years in the gold mines of California, where we went through all the ups and downs of a miner's life, made us very slow in giving credit to the gold stories which had been coming in all winter, and equally slow in believing stories to the contrary and which have caused the present panic among the Pike's Peakers. It appears that the panic is mostly on the route north of the Platte. On other routes a few returned, but the greater part continued to press on. . . . We advise no one to jump out of his boots and start off barefoot for the land of gold, but to wait for confirmation of the news.[21]

NINE

The Civil War Years

EDMUND'S views on slavery had many roots. He first became sensitive to the slavery issue while a young student at the Hartford school. Thomas Hopkins Gallaudet, the first director of the school, and Laurent Clerc, the head teacher, were outspoken and active opponents of slavery. Gallaudet had assisted in securing the freedom of a Moorish prince who had been sold into slavery. Both Gallaudet and Clerc were involved in the pretrial proceedings of the Africans who had rebelled on the slave ship *Amistad*. Edmund's first teachers likely inculcated strong beliefs in the rights of blacks to be free.

Several of Mary Ann's brothers had long been abolitionists. William Harrison ("Harry") Walworth was known for his fiery advocacy. In 1837, George helped to defend Elijah Lovejoy, the Presbyterian minister from Maine, who had condemned the lynching of a black man. George was with Lovejoy in Alton, Illinois, when a proslavery mob took Lovejoy's life and dumped his printing press into the river. Mary Ann herself was with her family in Alton when the tragic murder happened, only a short time before the Walworths moved to Buffalo Forks. John E. Lovejoy, the founder of the *Eureka*, was Elijah's brother, and Edmund knew him well.

Edmund's own intensive reading on the subject of slavery gave him a deep understanding of the issues. He admired Wendell Phillips, a Boston abolitionist who argued brilliantly for both emancipation and freedom of the press. Phillips had thanked the "little band at Alton for resisting those who threatened their rights to freedom of speech and insulted the law that many had fought so hard for during the Revolution."[1]

Edmund had read of the Fugitive Slave Act and the expanding Underground Railroad while he was in California. He discussed Harriet Beecher Stowe's book, *Uncle Tom's Cabin*, in his letters to Mary Ann and Thomas in 1852. In 1856, he was back home in Anamosa when John Brown and his followers murdered five southern settlers at Pottowatomie Creek in the Kansas Territory. Shortly after this, Edmund began writing for the *Eureka*, and with Crockwell he published spirited antislavery editorials. His 1858 "Carrier's Address" (see pp. 118–19) epitomized his sentiments as the tensions divided the country. When South Carolina seceded from the United States in late-December 1860, following Abraham Lincoln's victory in the November election, Edmund's loyalty to the Union surfaced immediately. In the *Eureka*, he called President Buchanan a "consummate coward . . . in full complicity with the conspirators." He wrote, "We have elected Lincoln 'according to the Constitution of the United States,' and we stand and will stand by that until the 4th of March, when the new President will be inaugurated and the plotters of treason will be overthrown. The Union will live on and South Carolina will be in it."[2]

Edmund also saw the economic motivation to the unrest in the South. When South Carolina declared herself out of the Union, he published an editorial in the *Eureka* and in which he asked, "What is the real cause of all this uproar in the South?" He believed that the answer was the southerners desire to reopen the slave trade. "Cotton culture is profitable business, but a slave, bought in a border state, costs $800 to $1200, and the same could be obtained from Africa for $200. This is the chief ransom and the main spring of all their action."[3]

In February 1861, Edmund wrote an editorial lambasting the Southern states for their secession.

No man can play such tom-foolery in a household, as our slave masters have played for forty years, without the other members asking the question: "What is that noisy, thieving fellow worth?" So it has been and when South Carolina and another and another went out, we could hardly believe them such utter blockheads, so thoroughly and hopelessly blind, as to go in earnest. . . . The slaveholders are, as is often the case with knaves, shrewd and sharp but shortsighted. They ignore utterly the fact that the generality of mankind have some degree of conscience, honor and common sense. In going out they go as robbers. They seize the common property wherever they can do so with safety, and on the Mississippi they place cannon and say to passing boats, "stand and deliver" wharf rates. . . . Slavery has elevated the negro and sunk the moral sense of the white man almost to nothing.[4]

Thanks to Edmund's detailed reporting, the *Eureka* archives contain rich accounts of Iowa's participation in the Civil War. On April 26, 1861, Edmund published in his "Home Matters" column a call by Governor Kirkwood for volunteers in the Iowa Regiments. "Rifles, Attention!" ran the headline. "It is desirable that it should be a crack corps and composed wholly of picked men. . . . between the ages of 18 and 45, who desire to serve their country in the present crisis." Edmund then wrote, "Citizens of Jones County! This call is addressed to you not as Republicans or Democrats, but as men who live the government under which they were born and have lived, and who are willing to fight for its support. . . . Let us have a company of Jones County 'picked men' of whom every one shall be a man to boast of in after years."[5]

Edmund did not hesitate to attack editors of other Iowa newspapers who sided with the South. "The Dubuque Herald," he wrote, is "at heart a secession paper and under the influence of such men as the traitor Ben M. Samuels who, a few weeks ago, openly advocated the secession of Iowa into the arms of Jeff Davis."[6]

By August, bands of rebels from Missouri were attacking near Chicauqua, Iowa, prompting pleas for help from Burlington. Even though the Iowa legislature had passed a bill to raise four regiments, no arms or ammunition had yet been obtained, and the superintendent of the Burlington and Missouri Railroad could only start an extra train with "what men and arms can be gathered here."[7]

Many of the companies formed in Iowa reported to Fort Randall in the Dakota Territory and eventually became part of a cavalry regiment sent in November 1861 to St. Louis for training. Some of these soldiers died of pneumonia and measles. Others were ordered to join General Grant's army in skirmishes against the Confederates.

The Eureka Printing Office was located on the second floor of this building on the corner of Main and Ford streets. Edmund Booth is seen standing in the doorway. Courtesy of Helen Heckenlaible and Wilma Spice.

Edmund covered the Civil War in great depth through articles reprinted from other newspapers. He kept his readers informed of the reactions to Jefferson Davis's creation of the Confederate States of America, how the War was financed, troop movements, Clara Barton's work, and many other events as they unfolded. He summarized battles in various states, especially those involving Iowa men. He regularly published letters from Iowa soldiers on the battlefronts. The letters were often addressed to "Friend Booth." L. Schoonover wrote a letter from Camp Warren at Burlington "in fulfillment of a promise which I made to you before leaving Jones County . . . I have leaned myself against a pile of boards, pen in hand and paper before me, for the purpose of informing you of some of the incidents of camp life." Schoonover was one of many soldiers who reported their war experiences to "Friend Booth." He was among 800 men and the

same number of horses in this camp. They were expecting about 1,200 in
a few days. "We have no arms yet," Schoonover told Edmund, "and what
drilling we do is on foot."[8] The Iowa men were often war-weary but determined to win. Their lengthy weekly letters read like entries in a diary.
Another soldier wrote to Edmund,

> The Jones County boys are all well . . . There is considerable sickness in
> camp, caused, I think, principally by the great heat of the past few days. . . .
> Perhaps there never was a company of men of more different occupations
> gathered together than there are in our regiment. We are composed of old
> and young, married and single, some farmers, some mechanics, some crafts-
> men, a goodly number of teachers, some doctors, preachers, lawyers, and all
> other professions. Over there is a man who spent five years in the British
> service in southern Africa; yonder is another who was through the Florida
> and Mexican wars; here is a man who was driven with his family from Mis-
> souri, who left his wife in Hopkinton and enlisted in the cavalry. Close by
> him is a native Mississippian who deserted from Jeff Davis' army after drilling
> three months, and several of our regiment have brothers in the southern
> army.[9]

The "correspondents," as Edmund called them, shared detailed reports
of skirmishes, such as the one at Athens, Missouri, where about 500 federal troops routed an equal number of rebels. They described how they
kept themselves busy in camps. One soldier wrote of his battalion leaving
St. Louis and camping at Jefferson City, where about half the houses were
vacant and some were used as hospitals for sick soldiers. After dark, a black
man whose master was a secessionist came into camp and told them where
to look for chickens, apples, cider, and other supplies. A postmaster was
arrested for not mailing a large number of letters from the soldiers.

In return, the soldiers found great pleasure in receiving the *Eureka*. "By
the way," one soldier wrote to Edmund, "you can have no conception of
the avidity with which letters and newspapers are literally devoured. Since
I have been here I have received The Eureka, and every boy from Jones
Co. has to have a sight of it."[10] Edmund also wrote back to many of the
men in the camps. They often assigned themselves such noms de plume as

"Supernumerary," "Quill Drive," and "Leonidas." Another soldier wrote in March 1862,

> This is mail day. "Has the Eureka come?" "Did you get the Anamosa Eureka this week?" are questions asked me on every side. Your paper is not only eagerly sought after by the Jones Co. boys, but is becoming a favorite with the others. The "Army Correspondence," particularly the letters from the 14th Regiment, are anxiously looked for, and when the writer states that there is a probability of their taking the field, the exclamations, "I wish we were with them," "I would give my bounty to join the remainder of regiment," etc, are heard on every side.[11]

Not much is known about the Booth's family life during the war. Thomas was studying in New Hampshire at the Kimball Union Academy during the start of the war. With two of their three children at home, Mary Ann and Edmund were kept busy. They had also donated land for the First Congregational Church. By Christmas 1861 the building was about finished and a service was held. Edmund noted that the interior looked fine, but building materials still littered the yard. In a letter to Thomas, Edmund mentioned that Hattie and some relatives had taken a sleigh ride on about an inch of snow to Waubeck to visit Danforth. The Booths spent Christmas by having a turkey brought by someone in payment for a subscription to the *Eureka*. A deaf guest, possibly Lewis Perkins, was also there. Hattie also wrote to Thomas, and Edmund warned his son that her letter writing contained many errors, which he would need to correct in the future.

Frank's boyhood was a healthy mix of work and play. Edmund predicted that Frank would be a sensible as well as energetic man. Thomas had given Frank a sled and, when out of school, Frank made abundant use of it, sliding downhill in the old pasture. He also enjoyed baseball, croquet, and skating. Edmund taught him to saw wood, split kindling, and bring it in and lay it by the stove for morning.

In December 1862, Edmund bought the remaining half interest in the *Eureka* and became the sole owner. Shortly after this, Thomas returned from New Hampshire and took on responsibilities in the composing room and as local manager. Frank had begun studying that year in a private school, where he learned to read. At the age of 7, he also began setting type in his father's printing business, working on Saturdays while other children his age were playing. Edmund and his sons must have shared many touching moments as they prepared their weekly newspaper, reading carefully as they set the type for such letters as the long tribute written by "Leonidas" to his comrades after batteries of Company B of the Iowa 9th Regiment had unsuccessfully stormed rebel troops on May 22, 1863. "It is fitting and just," Leonidas wrote, "that something should be said of these fallen and departed braves; that the memory of them and their heroic actions should be kept, preserved and embalmed in the hearts of the survivors, not only of the present but the future generations."[12]

The Emancipation Proclamation, signed by Abraham Lincoln on January 1, 1863, not only strengthened the president's position in the Republican Party, but freed hundreds of thousands of slaves in Confederate territory, many of whom joined the army to fight the Rebels. Edmund kept his readers informed of their experiences with letters such as the following from a white officer at Milliken's Bend, where there was a camp of the 11th Louisiana Infantry of African Descent.

Friend Booth:

You are well supplied with Army Correspondence from white Regiments, and this is one reason why I have not yet fulfilled my promise to write to you, thinking that there are men better able to write for newspapers than I am, but . . . I believe it to be of some interest to you and your readers to hear from the African Bridgade. A great deal has been said and written about the awful idea of organizing negro regiments, and men, who have promulgated that idea, have been cursed by some and highly applauded by others, according to the mental caliber of their critics, and all I have to say to those who oppose this enterprise is they must be either knaves or fools, because I do verily believe, first: that negroes ought to help fight the battles of this war, and should have been in service a year ago; it is their right and duty to do so, and they are willing to perform that duty. . . . Two days after we arrived here with our green or black force of about 700 men, partly armed and poorly drilled, some of whom had never fired a gun in their lives, we were attacked by a rebel force of 2,500 Texans under B.G. McCulloch, a brother of the famous Ben. McCulloch. On the 6th day of June, Sunday morning at three o'clock, the attack was made simultaneously on three points, under Major General W.T. Walker, C.S.A., commanding. . . . I cannot speak in too high praise of the conduct of our black soldiers on that memorable day, and I am far from being an enthusiast, but I like to see justice done to the so much abused African race; they have given proofs to the world that they can and will fight.[13]

In all, more than 76,000 soldiers from Iowa fought in the Civil War, including 440 black soldiers; 337 officers and 13,252 enlisted men were killed in battle or died of wounds, disease, or from other causes. In the years following the war, the *Anamosa Eureka* published lists of the soldiers' names with descriptions of how they died. Edmund knew many of the men who died, including Daniel and Harrison Joslin, the sons of John G. Joslin, who had performed the Booths' wedding ceremony. Edmund's correspondence with the surviving soldiers established friendships that lasted for many years. One such soldier, John C. Magee of Tulsa, Oklahoma, later wrote the following letter to the Reverend F. P. Shaffer of the Methodist church in Anamosa:

I lived on a farm in Scotch Grove township, Jones county, when a boy. It was 14 miles northeast of Anamosa. We took the Eureka, Edmund Booth, editor. He was a mute, whether by birth or injury I do not know. He was smart and made a good paper. While I was in the army I wrote some letters to the Eureka over the nom de plume of "High Private." I had never met the old gentleman. When I got home I was in Anamosa one day, called on him and wrote "High Private" on a piece of paper. He laughed, shook my hand cordially, almost hugged me and took off my hat, which I, shy in my manners, I suppose, had not removed. He looked over my head, or my head over. I do not know what he thought, but he said some kind words and was cheerily companionable.[14]

Edmund had an odd habit of examining the heads of any person he found interesting. He was a long-time believer in phrenology, the theory developed by Franz Joseph Gall in the eighteenth century that aspects of a person's personality and intellect might be explained from the shape of his head. As early as 1844, when Thomas was a young boy, Edmund had studied his own son's head in this manner: "I knew he would rise above common (from his head and size of lungs)," he had written to Mary Ann while she was staying with her parents in Illinois, "but I feared at times that it might be a father's partiality."[15]

Thomas also knew Magee, and he remembered that "Father, without doubt, made some remarks along phrenological lines, but probably was not clearly understood by Mr. Magee, as his speech was not always readily understood, and so [Magee] does not recollect anything except the general purport and manner of his greeting. The statement by Mr. Magee that he was nearly "hugged" by the Senior indicated his affection for him and the boys in blue generally."[16]

EDMUND Booth's papers contain no mention that he was directly involved in the Underground Railroad. Nevertheless, Thomas Milner, an Iowa farm boy who later became an attorney, described Edmund, as well as his own father, as "black Abolitionists" who "were never so happy as when they were violating the iniquitous and cursed Fugitive Slave Law."[17] Edmund used his editorials to express his outrage with the southern states. "Under the circumstances," he wrote, "peaceable secession is out of the question. They must be made to feel that the North is a power which it is not safe to provoke." He boldly called for a "sound drubbing" of the "southern blusterers. . . . There can be no permanent peace till the rebellious slaveholders are completely overthrown and reduced to submission."[18]

Throughout the Civil War Edmund attacked the "Copperheads," those in the North who were southern sympathizers, some so proud of their label that they wore badges made from copper pennies. Harriet remembered her father's courage in the midst of intense political harassment.

His pen spared no one. He hated a "copperhead" with all his might, and they hated him. He could not be bluffed or [intimidated]. Mother shared father's feelings, but when threatening letters came to him, she was much worried. Father enjoyed them. After receiving these warnings, when he met a democrat or "copperhead" on the street, he would pull out one such letter, read it to him, then throw back his head and laugh. The man couldn't "talk back," so father had it all his own way. Father demonstrated that "the pen is mightier than the sword." He did more for the Union than any one soldier excepting only a Grant or a Sherman or a Sheridan.[19]

In June 1863, Edmund attacked the Copperheads again in the *Eureka*, this time for their insistence on the right of free speech.

For thirty years the slaveholders have hanged, imprisoned and exiled men and women for exercising that right of free speech, and northern proslaveryites, in State and Church, had nothing to say; and not only so but these same proslaveryites aided in the work, mobbing, stoning, rotten-egging, tarring, feathering and riding on rails those who in the North ventured to exercise the right of free speech against the divine (!?) institution, and masters' right to daily, openly and outrageously violate every one of the . . . commandments. . . . but how is it with . . . the many thousands of Union men and women in the South? Are *they* allowed free speech? Not an iota, but catch a Copperhead condemning anything done or said by Jeff. & Co.![20]

Edmund's sometimes overly dramatic editorials would lead to arguments with his opponents on the street. The emotions he experienced during these verbal exchanges with Copperheads would cause his voice, which he had difficulty controlling, to rise to a high pitch. At times it was so loud that Thomas could hear it from a distance, and Edmund's antagonists found it useless to reply to the deaf man.

I heard father called a 'black abolitionist' more than once, though he was generally held in high esteem personally, but the Democrats especially, and some Whigs, later Republicans, had little love for his blind advocacy of abolition doctrines. Some of his poetic expressions are touched with the fire of his hatred for the man-selling system and the doughfaces north and south who supported it . . . Father's love for the Union cause and the boys in blue was remarkable, and especially those who went from this county, and they loved him in return. The political struggles . . . were characterized by great bitterness, sometimes dangerously near bursting into the flames of civil strife, and now and then involving actual personal conflict. Father's pen during the war spared not the country's enemies, whether southern or northern rebels. But when the final victory came, with the curse of slavery swept away and the Union saved, father said that he felt that his work was done. And it was, in a large and essential degree.[21]

Edmund had an unswerving belief that the Union would prevail. Hattie recalled that, "It seemed sometimes that his whole being was afire. His indignation and anger against those who were opposing or plotting against the government was strong and deep."[22] He was a great admirer of William Lloyd Garrison, and Edmund patterned the masthead of the *Eureka* after one of Garrison's strongest edicts—"NO COMPROMISE WITH SLAVERY! NO UNION WITH SLAVEHOLDERS!"[23] In September 1863, Edmund changed his masthead to "No Compromise Under Menace: No Surrender of Principles; No Concession to Traitors."

The message behind Edmund's *Eureka* editorials was, "My opinions will be *read*." Toward this goal, he became increasingly enthusiastic as the war neared its end. On February 23, 1865, as he reported on the evacuation of Charleston, he ran the headline, "John Brown's Soul Is Marching On!"[24] A month later, he wrote that "the Confederacy is nearly ready for its grand tumble. It was built through lies and deception and founded on a great, in fact a most stupendous lie—the lie man might own his fellow—that the capitalist might and ought to own the laborer."[25]

When Robert E. Lee surrendered at Appomattox, Virginia, Edmund noted how impossible it was "to do justice to this matter in an ordinary newspaper article. . . . The Southern world is turned upside down with a vengeance and its bondmen are its masters."[26]

In the next issue, Edmund wrote of the "horrible murder" of President Abraham Lincoln, "another of the many evidences of the depth of barbarian fiendishness to which slavery reduces its votaries."[27] Edmund was visibly upset by Lincoln's death. When he came home to tell his family the news, "his face was white and stern. The lines about his mouth were set and his eye expressed both deep anger and sorrow."[28] The cause for which he had argued so passionately had been won at a terrible cost.

TEN

Raising a Family

ANAMOSA grew slowly during the Civil War. Railroad cars had been rolling into the "uptown" depot since 1860. In 1865, the telegraph finally went into operation in Anamosa. "Eureka!" Edmund wrote, "We are in lightning communication with the Universe!"[1] These advances in transportation and telecommunications, as well as the end of the Civil War, helped to accelerate the growth of the town. At the northeast corner of the block that had been Edmund Booth's potato patch now stood the Congregational Society's church. This land, which he donated to the Society in 1861, eventually became one of the most important public blocks in Anamosa, the site of the post office, fire department, public library, and other businesses.

Although the war was over, Edmund took no hiatus in his attacks on slavery. He proudly wrote in 1866, "we [the *Eureka*] have advocated, openly, plainly, determinedly, the abolition of slavery and in this ours was, up to the breaking out of the rebellion and so far as we know, the most openly and persistently radical paper in the State. Pro-slaveryites held up their hands and rolled their eyes in horror at our utterances, and timid Republicans protested against carrying the subject to such extremes. . . . Both Houses of the Iowa Legislature have voted, and voted unanimously, for the amendment to the U.S. Constitution abolishing slavery. . . . Here is a triumph worth ten years of labor."[2] In issue after issue, the *Eureka* reported on the aftermath of the war, including the capture of Jefferson

Davis, speeches by Frederick Douglass, and the federal government's approach to Reconstruction under Andrew Johnson. The *Eureka* also proposed that a monument be erected in the old cemetery to formally remember the soldiers who gave their lives in the Civil War.[3]

THE Booth family prospered during the decade following the Civil War. The three children, all able to communicate with Edmund and Mary Ann in signs, were nurtured well, physically and spiritually. Thomas and Hattie were now young adults. On May 18, 1868, Thomas married Gertrude Delavan in Hopkinton, Iowa. In addition to his work with the *Eureka*, Thomas became very active in the First Congregational Church. He served as a deacon and trustee, a Sunday school superintendent, a teacher of the adult Bible class, and a member of the choir. He also served on the Anamosa cemetery board and was a strong temperance worker. Like his father, he did not shrink from defending his views in the *Eureka*. He emulated Edmund's excellence in editorial work, especially honesty and in his love for humanity. Gertrude was a teacher. For years, she also helped with the *Eureka*, especially the sections reporting on local news and events.

Soon after Thomas and Gertrude's wedding, Mary Ann traveled east for the summer to visit Hattie, who was then studying at Mt. Holyoke College (South Hadley Seminary) in Springfield, Massachusetts. Mt. Holyoke had about 260 students at the time, and 24 teachers. The basic expenses per year were $150, but fuel, lights, and lectures cost extra. Hattie had previously attended the Kimball Union Academy, just as Thomas had done earlier, and over a period of four years she spent vacations and summers at the house of Elisha T. Parsons, a family friend, or with Mary Ann's brother, James. Her Uncle James was an adventurous type, too. During one vacation, he invited Hattie to ride with him behind his fast trotter and when a train came by, from Newtonville to Newton Center, he raced it neck and neck. "It nearly took my breath away," she wrote.[4] Hattie's cousin, Arthur, who was studying at Yale, also spent vacations there, and the two of them took many long horseback rides around the Boston countryside.

In the summer of 1868, Mary Ann went with Hattie to the Mt. Holyoke campus, where, Hattie wrote, she "attracted considerable attention and I was proud of her."[5] Mary Ann then traveled to her birthplace, Canaan, New Hampshire. While there, she was none too happy to learn that Frank had injured his foot in an accident with a pitchfork back home. Mary Ann grabbed the motherly opportunity to admonish Edmund to exercise more caution with their son. "When I was at home," she told him, "I always took care of them lest Frank might get hurt." She also insisted that he put the pitchfork out of reach.[6]

While visiting with relatives, Mary Ann went to see the home where she had lived as a child. The house, now vacant, had not changed much, except the outside had been repaired and painted. In her letter to Edmund, she reported that she "looked for everything which remind me that I felt sad that I had parted with my parents, brothers and sisters with whom I used to live together happily and that they were scattered to a distance from each other." She also visited the cemetery where her grandparents were buried. "There were many nice and white tombs where you remember that you and myself went up to visit when you came from Hartford to see me," she told Edmund. She met a man who remembered her when she was a child, and he shook hands with her warmly and "said that I looked like my father exactly." Neighbors who remembered her then gathered together, eager to learn about her life in Iowa. She visited with friends she had gone to school with in Canaan before she went to Hartford, and she enjoyed riding around the orchard where she grew up. She told Edmund that on her way to a Shaker meeting, she took "the same road where you and myself rode on the horseback to Enfield and we were lost!"[7]

During this visit, Mary Ann also went with relatives to the graveyard in Canaan where her sister Eunice and her nephew were buried. Her brother Clark's wife came to Canaan and brought her to Boston for a visit. She ended her letter to Edmund by sending a "thousand kisses" to Frank and once again warning her husband, "you must take care of him don't let him stay in the evenings in the streets."[8]

Hattie became ill in the spring of 1870, and returned home to Anamosa so her family could take care of her. Mary Ann soon afterwards came home to Iowa to be with her. By the fall, Hattie had improved, and she began teaching at Lenox Collegiate Institute in Hopkinton, Iowa. She continued in that position until her marriage to George F. LeClere, a Presbyterian minister, in 1875.

The education system in Anamosa had improved with time. Frank studied grammar, physiology, rhetoric, and algebra, while in high school. After graduating in 1872, he entered Iowa State College in the spring of 1873. He worked on the school's farm several hours per day to earn expenses, but he had to leave after his first year because his parents could not afford the tuition. Frank took a job at a printing office in Chicago for several months, and then he returned home to work in the *Anamosa Eureka* printing office. By the spring of 1875 he was able to reenter college. He graduated in 1877. While in college, Frank was in charge of the college printing office; his salary covered all of his expenses so that his parents were not burdened by the costs. He earned enough money to travel to the Centennial Exposition in Philadelphia in 1876. It was at that Exposition that Alexander Graham Bell first demonstrated his telephone.

BY THE early 1870s, Anamosa had become a sizable village. An immense quantity of limestone rock on both sides of the Wapsipinicon River provided a great resource for the town, which served as the seat of Jones County. Many farms covered the spacious prairie around Anamosa. Mary Ann's house, built in a cornfield in the early 1850s while Edmund was in the California gold mines, served as the Booth family homestead until 1869. Thomas and Gertrude lived in that house for several more years after that.[9] Edmund and Mary Ann built a home on South Ford Street in 1870. Edmund transplanted three apple trees, which Mary Ann had started a few years earlier from seeds taken from some fine apples. The family enjoyed the blossoms and applesauce for many years afterwards.

Edmund and Mary Ann became grandparents in July 1871, when a daughter, Bertha May, was born to Thomas and Gertrude. In December 1872, a second daughter, Mabel Gertrude, was born. Mary Ann devoted her time to managing the home and overseeing the expanding family.

For many years, Edmund and Thomas Booth argued in *Anamosa Eureka* editorials for the establishment of a fire company in Anamosa. The Weir Hook & Ladder Company was finally formed in the late 1870s. The 75 men of the fire company often marched in town parades dressed in their uniforms. At the upper right corner of the photograph stands the Booth house on Ford Street. Courtesy of the Paul C. Juhl Collection, State Historical Society of Iowa.

Throughout the years, she entertained the grandchildren with her re-sourcefulness at such games as "blindman's buff," where she was "the queen of the flying squad of buffens and could slip out of a tight corner and elude the out-reaching arms of the most active 'blind' man with a dexterity unsurpassed and unsurpassable." She was always a "marvel of activity."[10] Any time the grandchildren were hungry, they approached Grandma Booth with their rudimentary sign language skills, knowing that she would come to the rescue. As Thomas reminisced, "I can see their impetuous, smiling signs right now—slice of bread, butter spread over, and molasses—index finger drawn persuasively through red lips—pouring round and round. . . . Mother understood it all before the sweet petition in pantomime was presented."[11]

While studying at Iowa State College in 1873, Frank received a letter from his father, which revealed how busy Edmund, then 63 years old, was keeping himself with the newspaper work, family, and gardening. He described planting lettuce and beets, parsnips and peas "abundantly because Clark & family may be here and for Tom if he does not get his garden in order in time." He tied up grapevines to frames and transplanted an asparagus bed to the north side of the garden along the fence. He told Frank that Hattie's vacation from her teaching post was beginning on June 10, "the day of the meeting of the Editors' convention at Cedar Rapids." He mentioned plans to travel to Ames, Iowa, on the Northwestern railroad.[12]

IN 1866, the Booths bought new power presses, but their office space was too small to hold all the equipment. It was also too dark, especially for an editor who was blind in one eye. Edmund moved the *Eureka* to the second floor of a new building on the corner of Main and Ford streets. A hardware store occupied the first floor. The main room in the new building measured 26 × 60 feet, with windows looking out on both Main Street and Ford Street. The two back rooms were 10 × 12 feet. Prior to moving the presses to the new space, Edmund reported in the *Eureka* that "the weight of material to be moved is not less than six tons. Ugh!"[13]

Thomas began working for the *Eureka*, in the late 1850s, while he was still a student. Over the course of his career, he served as a foreman, job printer, local manager, and editor. He also was responsible for the roller department, helping to put out 400 copies of the newspaper each week. When the *Eureka* expanded to an 8-column format, with a total of 32 columns, the publication day changed from every Friday to every Thursday. The masthead read "The Anamosa Eureka" and under that "Independent in Everything." In October 1867, Thomas bought a half interest in the paper and the company name became E. Booth & Son, with no changes in the management. At this point, Thomas stopped doing the heavy work and focused more on writing. The *Anamosa Eureka* became even more prosperous and was the leading official weekly of Jones County.

Through the years, reports on train accidents, collapsed hot air balloons, runaway teams of horses, the growth of business and industry, and a variety of other topics added human interest to the newspaper. Local issues often focused on farming concerns, including impurities in water, grain prices, poultry exhibits, and diseases carried by hogs. In 1873, the license tax on the sale of wine, beer, and ale was raised to $200. A tax of $100 was levied on each billiard table that saloons set up. Anamosa also passed a law that said anyone found drunk within city limits would be arrested and brought before the mayor or sheriff and fined $10 and the costs of whatever damages they caused in their drunken state.

Edmund's interest in temperance never abated throughout his life. However, many of Anamosa's citizens did not share his convictions. Even Anamosa's governing council ignored the 1855 temperance law passed by the state of Iowa. In reaction, many townswomen took up hatchets and axes and smashed whiskey barrels and decanters in an attempt to close down the saloons. By 1857, the *Eureka* was speaking out adamantly on this issue, "All this will account for the different drunken places that have sprung up lately in this place. The law says that all peace officers shall abate these nuisances and that drunken men shall be taken up and fined under a penalty of fine and forfeiture of office. Has any been abated? Has any been taken up? Not one!" By 1867, there were fourteen saloons in Anamosa![14]

Edmund and Thomas demonstrated a great sense of humor in some of the editorial battles with neighboring newspapers, especially the Marion *Register*. When the *Eureka* reported on the "scalawags, scoundrels, and liars" among the Marion railroad managers, the *Register* accused the *Eureka* editors of labeling the people of Marion as such.[15] In July 1871, the *Register* reported that "this world is entirely too troublesome for the venerable men who fill the chair editorial in the Anamosa *Eureka* and Maquoketa *Sentinel* offices. 'Happiness being the chief aim of man' they should have been in Heaven long ago. If they delay their 'Departure' much longer we are afraid they will 'dead head' it over the Midland to the 'other place.'" To which the Booths responded: "We hope that 'other place' won't be Marion. The torment there would be *ennui*."[16]

Among the issues that annoyed Edmund was the pronunciation of his town's name. Although profoundly deaf, he was aware that many people pronounced it An-a-moss-a, and more than once he reminded his readership of the long "o" in the third syllable.

Edmund frequently wrote on injustice and cruelty, and he was also bitterly opposed to mistreatment of any kind. He immersed himself in arguments with editors of other local newspapers on these subjects, including the killing of prairie chickens: "The chicken clubbers who shoot birds merely to gratify a coarse vanity and a brutish instinct of destructiveness ought to be placed in charge of the Society for Prevention of Cruelty to Animals. There is nothing high or praiseworthy in tearing birds with shot just to gratify such propensities. These clubbers need civilizing." When the *Dubuque Times* complained that "there is no use in arguing the point with the EUREKA; it is determined to have its way at all hazards," Edmund replied that he would let the attribution of poor motive pass.[17]

The newspaper became Edmund's platform to expound his views of the world. He used the *Eureka* not only for communicating with townspeople, but for advocating his political views and effecting change in society. A deaf man had little chance to succeed in politics in the nineteenth century. Edmund's speech was unnatural, and, without hearing, he could not effectively debate his views with opponents in any public forum. The printed word, especially in a newspaper he managed with his son, provided an opportune vehicle for communication with others. His advocacy on many fronts highlighted his leadership as a newspaper editor. He never shied away from expressing his opinions on a wide range of issues.

In the *Anamosa Eureka*, Edmund reported on international, national, state, and local issues, the latter in a column titled "Home Matters." He and Thomas covered corruption in state and national governments. They reported on Susan B. Anthony's crusade to obtain voting rights for women, the struggles of blacks during the postwar years to gain literacy, and wars in Europe. Readers continued to follow excellent coverage of

Reconstruction, the postwar activities of Jefferson Davis, the work of the Freedmen's Bureau, investigations by the Judiciary Committee of the assassination of Abraham Lincoln, and the impeachment of Andrew Johnson. The Booths also reprinted articles from such newspapers as the *New York Tribune, Dubuque Times, Monticello Express, Boston Globe, Des Moines Republican*, and from periodicals such as *The Scientific American*.

Edmund fought hard for universal suffrage, which, he believed would "follow in the next generation if not sooner."[18] Thomas recognized that his father was a visionary, and believed that, "judging from the past, he saw the future with the eye of a prophet."[19] Many examples of this deaf man's foresight can be found in the *Eureka*. In April 1867, for example, Edmund wrote that "man will be far in advance of the present in arts, sciences and understanding of Nature's laws." In May that year he commented that the eight-hour workday newly in effect in Illinois showed the positive direction to which society was tending.

Edmund continued to fight for the rights of black people. In 1857, Jones County residents had voted 1,000 to 300 against granting black men the right to vote. A decade later, Edmund urged residents to support this right.

> Iowa is ready and so is New York . . . because a different course is hopeless. . . . The time, however, has now come, and all Congress has to do is to put public sentiment into the shape of law and also give the States an opportunity to embody it in the constitution. Joshua might command the sun and moon to stand still, but there never lived and never will live a Joshua able to stop the triumphant march of mankind toward the millennium.[20]

He countered arguments in other newspapers that claimed black men were unfit to vote.

> The *New York World* has the impudence to assert, four years after the war of the rebellion has ended, that the colored people of this country are morally unfit for citizenship, because, according to the census of 1860, thirty-six percent of them are mulattoes, mostly born out of wedlock. This fact it regards as conclusive evidence of the gross immorality of the colored women. Since the bulk of the colored people resided in the South in 1860,

where their marriage was not recognized by law, and since for this gross injustice the white paramours of helpless black women were alone responsible, it strikes us that the logical result of the *World's* argument is that Southern whites, and not their late slaves, are morally incapacitated for the rights of citizenship.[21]

In an article in the *Annals of Iowa* in 1871, he reminisced about the early years of Iowa, still bitter over how the United States census in 1840 had been biased in favor of slavery. Later that year he continued to attack the Ku Klux Klan. In February 1872, he attracted the attention of the *Eureka* readers with the headline, "The Ku Klux are coming!" He then followed this with, "but they won't be dangerous. Twenty four of these misguided Southerners, who whip and shoot negroes for fun, have arrived at the Albany Penitentiary. . . . They belong to the most unattractive of the 'white trash' of the South."[22]

> Today the southern Democracy and the Ku Klux are of one mind and their ideas run in the old rut. Give them power and they will, as near as possible, bring back the old order of things. . . . The party which conquered the rebellion and saved the nation must hold its ground. The ex-slave masters do not change. . . . Time and a new generation are needed to render permanent the present constitutional statues. A race of men in the South must grow up to the conditions of this new era.[23]

In support of women's suffrage, Edmund reprinted an article from the *Independent,* another Iowa newspaper, that said women were the best advocates for their own rights. The article mentions Harriet Martineau, a deaf writer, one of the signers of a letter of sympathy to the Second National Woman's Rights Convention. The author of the article noted that men had had advocated for women's suffrage up until the present time. Edmund felt proud to be a part of that very tradition. He commented that Iowa had one female lawyer, Mrs. Mary E. Magoon, and he saw no reason why women could not be lawyers. When the *Independence Bulletin* and *State Register* newspapers stated that they were the first papers in Iowa to advocate women's suffrage, Edmund retorted,

The *Eureka* openly, decidedly, and bluntly, and when, like abolition, the very name was 'odious,' advocated woman's suffrage before the *Bulletin* saw the light, before the *Des Moines Citizen* was transmogrified into the *State Register*, and probably while the editors of those papers were far away east of the big Daddy of waters and under the school-master's birch. We have said little on the subject of late. The battle is won and we leave the eleventh hour men to finish off the struggle, gather up the wounded and bury the dead; only their wrangling over the question of priority is comical, not in itself, but when we remember the fierce and gloomy past.[24]

In addressing the mistreatment of women and people of color, Edmund was the master of persuasion. He held a bond with other marginalized people and he continually spoke out for their rights. As a deaf man, he lived in two worlds and was very successful in both.

ELEVEN

The Deaf Community

𝕽𝕾𝕻𝕽

AS A former schoolteacher, Edmund remained interested in the welfare of deaf children throughout his life. His interest extended to any and every deaf person he could locate in his region as well. As soon as he learned of families who had deaf members, he would make the trek to establish ties.

Although he lived on the frontier plains for more than six decades, Edmund Booth became an icon in the American Deaf community during his own lifetime. He taught in Hartford for only a few years, yet he was held up as a pioneering educator of deaf pupils. In his book, *The Abbé de l'Epée, Founder of the Manual Instruction of the Deaf, and Other Early Teachers of the Deaf,* Edwin Isaac Holycross included Edmund Booth along with the "Three Immortals," Epée, Thomas Hopkins Gallaudet, and Laurent Clerc, as a reason why "sign language will never be a dead language." Holycross emphasized Booth's "sturdy courage" and "intellectual brightness" that "exercised so powerful an impetus upon the welfare of the deaf upon the progress of the community wherein was reopened the harvest of his riper years and larger experience."[1]

Edmund Booth's courage and intellect were indeed the stuff of legends. His fellow deaf and hearing teachers, as well as his pupils, whom he taught for seven years, followed his whereabouts and his accomplishments through reports in the early newspapers of the Deaf community and in the *American Annals of the Deaf and Dumb,* the primary periodical for educators of deaf students. Reports about Edmund also appeared in the *Association Review,* a journal edited by his son, Frank. Edmund's voluminous correspondence, most of it now lost, included exchanges with former colleagues in Hartford and other towns. The accumulated effects of his early experience as one of the nation's first deaf teachers, his efforts to support the establishment of several schools for deaf children, his mature perspectives published in the *American Annals* regarding instruction, the debate over a Deaf commonwealth, and other topics, and his reputation as a deaf frontiersman who shrank at no challenge in the larger community of hearing people, earned him well-deserved respect over time. By his seventh decade, Edmund was an elder spokesman of the Deaf community, and neither distance nor the isolation imposed by life on the prairie frontier lessened this status. After his lecture to the Clerc Literary Association in 1901, he was referred to as "an honored nestor" of the Deaf community by a writer in *The Silent Worker,* who also wrote, "age has not . . . abated one jot or tittle the particular interest he has ever felt in the doings of the deaf world, and the throng that gathered in the chapel of All Soul's Church a week since was repaid by a talk that was a piece de resistance of the season."[2] Edmund was later revered for his use of "sign language in its purity and clearness" and, with artist/poet John Carlin and painter H. Humphrey Moore, he was considered among those who should be included in a proposed American Deaf community's "Temple of Fame."[3]

The Deaf community began to coalesce and create its own organizations in the mid-nineteenth century. St. Ann's Church for the Deaf formed in 1852 in New York to provide deaf people with a place to attend services in sign language. In 1854, the New England Gallaudet Association became the first organization established by deaf people for deaf people. Many of the early members had attended the American School in Hartford. Edmund was in California when these developments occurred, but it did not take him long to catch up on the news after he returned to Iowa. In 1858 he published an article in the *American Annals* counseling deaf people in the East to be cautious before rushing to the West. Iowa alone was growing at an annual rate of 100,000; by 1858 the population was more than 600,000. Looking back on his eighteen years in Iowa and California, he cautioned the Deaf community that "a frontier life is not. . . . a bed of roses," what with wolves and rattlesnakes and 5-mile trips for firewood or fencing material. "Brethren! If you have farms that are productive, and are thus or otherwise well off, or have aged parents who depend on you, I cannot say, come West."[4] Edmund read other newspapers for glimpses of the human experience to share with the *Eureka*'s readership. When he found tidbits about deafness, he would include them in his own newspaper. He published, without comment, an article titled, "Why Cousins Should Not Marry," which he extracted from the annual report of the Kentucky Institution for the Deaf and Dumb. This article presented conclusive arguments about the high incidence of deafness among children of such unions.[5] Edmund reported the tragic consequences of walking along railroad tracks, a common occurrence in many towns that did not have paved roads. The *Eureka* carried a story about a deaf woman named McClosky who failed to hear the train's warning and was killed.[6] She was one of hundreds of deaf people who died this way. From the *Des Moines Register*, Edmund reprinted a report about a family that had thirteen children, all of whom were deaf. "The family is a good one," he wrote, "and much respected in the community. We doubt if there is another family on this earth with as much silence in it as this."[7] In another issue, he published the announcement of the marriage of Mollie L. Church, a deaf woman, one of the "elite" of Memphis, and H. J. Haight of New Jersey, in an "impressive ceremony" that was "witnessed by the *bon ton* of the city."[8]

Despite Edmund's lifelong use of sign language, he never took a particularly strong stance when its use in the classroom was questioned and later suppressed throughout the country. In February 1869 he reprinted an article from the *Correspondence Chicago Advance* that described communication between deaf children and their parents. The article noted that most parents communicated with their deaf child not through "a well-guided and regular system of signs, but only by natural ones as the parents have learned from him. Thus he is at once child and teacher." In spite of the patronizing tone of the article, which referred to deaf people as "idiots" and "savages," and blamed their bad "conduct at home and in school" on parents who neglected to cultivate their child's mind, Edmund printed it without any comment. In another issue of the *Eureka*, Edmund reprinted an article from the *Chicago Advance* titled "Among the Mutes," in which the writer, in reporting his observations of a classroom, attributed the inappropriate combinations of words found in some deaf children's writing to the use of sign language. Edmund knew well that the inability to hear spoken language and the lack of practice with English could explain the observed writing errors, but he published the report without sharing his wisdom on the subject. Edmund himself was living proof that one can master sign language as well as written English with appropriate practice.[9]

Why Edmund passed up these opportunities to educate the public will never be known. He had a long-time interest in providing formal schooling for deaf children in Iowa. During his early years in Iowa, he was instrumental in convincing the legislature to send Iowa's deaf children to the Illinois Institution for Education of the Deaf and Dumb in Jacksonville. When he returned from California, he reconsidered this arrangement and realized "the time had come for a school of our own."[10] In 1854, he contacted the principal of the Jacksonville school to inquire about the number of pupils attending from Iowa. He also wrote to David E. Bartlett and encouraged him to come to Iowa City. Bartlett was a successful teacher and director of a school in Poughkeepsie, New York. He had taught with Edmund at the American Asylum and had the experience needed to establish a new school. Bartlett declined the invitation, however. Missouri and Louisiana recently had opened schools, and Texas was now exploring the idea. While he hoped for a school to be established in Iowa, Edmund knew it would be difficult to find a qualified leader.

Knowing no other teacher of mutes, outside of the regular institutions, worth having, and knowing also that no teacher, properly qualified, naturally or otherwise, and connected with any established institution, would sever such connection for what might appear a Don Quixotic adventure into a frontier state, and the up hill work of starting a new school . . . I concluded to wait until near the time of the assembling of the next Iowa legislature, and then by letter or in some way interest a few of the prominent men of Iowa City in the project, induce them to bring the matter before the legislature, and obtain an appropriation for the founding of an Iowa institution for the education of the deaf and dumb, to be located in the capital of the state. A foundation of this kind once laid, I knew there would not be the slightest difficulty in obtaining any one of the best teachers in the older institutions to take charge of it.[11]

Meanwhile, the Reverend William E. Ijams from the Illinois institution expressed interest in starting a school in Iowa. The Iowa legislature responded favorably to this news, and Ijams left Illinois in 1854 to begin the new school, which opened officially in 1855 in Iowa City with about twenty pupils. Shortly after it opened, Edmund paid a visit. He "enjoyed an old familiar chat in the language of signs, also making the acquaintance of Mr. Ijams."[12] Ijams did not remain at the school for long, though, and when he retired, Benjamin Talbot of the Ohio Institution for the Deaf became the principal.

A few years later, Dr. Nathan Sales, the mayor of Anamosa, met Edmund on the street and boastfully stated, "I expect the votes of all you mutes, for I am the father of the institution for the deaf and dumb." Edmund was miffed by this comment:

> The effrontery of the remark was, for the moment, astounding in its effect.
> He was the leader of his party—the democratic,—the war of the rebellion
> was raging, and I was the editor of the only republican journal in the county.
> As soon as I could recover, I replied: "I claim that honor; you was [sic] only
> my tool. If any other man had been in your place in the legislature, I should
> have sent my letters to him." He laughed, and admitted the justice of that
> view. . . . As to the honor . . . I had never given it a thought. Each had done
> his duty . . . and each ought to be satisfied, and certainly I was. To do
> him justice, he was, and is an awful politician . . . but is a good fellow in
> general."[13]

When the legislature proposed to erect a new building for the Iowa school, Edmund argued against the school being permanently located in Anamosa, as "public institutions are liable to mismanagement and abuse by those in charge."[14] He felt it was essential to have the school where the legislature and the state officers could follow its progress. In the 1870s, the school was moved to an 80-acre campus outside Council Bluffs.

EDMUND Booth became a nationally known voice of reason for deaf people in the mid-nineteenth century due to his participation in a public debate that lasted for several years. The debate began in 1855, when John Jacobus Flournoy, a deaf Georgian, distributed a pamphlet entitled "Scheme for a Commonwealth," in which he argued for the establishment of a deaf colony or state. Flournoy, who had briefly studied at the American Asylum in Hartford, and the University of Georgia, had tried several times to obtain a government position, but he was never successful.[15] Discouraged by inequality and the deprivation of basic rights and privileges that deaf people constantly faced, he proposed that deaf people set up their own state in the West, where hearing people could not take a leadership role in the government. He first approached William W. Turner, editor of the *American Annals of the Deaf and Dumb,* who subsequently questioned the practicality of pursuing such an idea. Turner considered it "beautiful in theory," but he argued in the *Annals* that it would be difficult to convince deaf people to leave the communities in which they now lived, and he questioned what would happen to all the children who were likely to be hearing.[16]

Like Edmund Booth, Flournoy was a "semi-mute" (deaf, but able to use his speech) and a capable writer himself. He was also an eccentric who wrote frequently to the newspapers in his home state on a variety of political and social issues. Much of Flournoy's writing in regard to deaf people contained a "peculiarity of thought and unsoundness of judgment."[17] Among his various remedies was the "deaf-mute colony," for which he advocated vehemently. On August 18, 1857, he wrote to Edmund about this idea, and Edmund responded on September 6, saying, "candidly that I hold it to be an impossibility, save in the commencement, and that on a very small scale."[18] Edmund shared his perspectives with Flournoy on the need for a variety of trades. He questioned how the commonwealth would deal with the mostly hearing children of deaf people, as well as many other concerns.

Flournoy became irritated by the "formidable objections" presented by Edmund Booth and William Turner. He argued that his proposal should be considered with a more philosophical view. On the issue of hearing children, he wrote that they "may not inherit land in that anomalous and contracted community—neither power nor patronage."[19] Deaf parents could supply their children with means to buy real estate in nearby states. Whether the colony succeeded or failed, Flournoy believed these deaf people would have proven that they "are capable of many things. . . . and may be treated as men and women of *some use* to society and to the country, and respected accordingly."[20]

Edmund was no stranger to dreams of separatism, even geographical. He was living in Iowa in 1846 when the first groups of Mormons settled temporarily in the southwestern part of the state. Later, he saw many of their wagon trains heading west as he made his way to California. He had studied and debated the plight of black people in the United States and was passionate in his feelings about abolishing slavery. As for deaf people, even he himself had entertained, with his young friends at the American Asylum in Hartford, the dream of a utopian society. But now he argued against the idea. He questioned Flournoy's perspectives on the happiness and welfare of deaf people. In the North and West, he explained, deaf people were perhaps more comfortable than in the South, where Flournoy lived. He also saw more to distinction than political office alone. As to Flournoy's plea to take a philosophical view of the proposal, Edmund's rebuttal centered on a discussion of constitutional rights, rights that he thought would be violated by any law constructed by deaf people that prohibited hearing people from voting or owning of land.[21] Edmund certainly understood the need of deaf people to be with others who shared the language of signs and the experiences of struggling to communicate with people who did not understand deafness. From the first day of his trek to California with Benjamin Clough to his final days mining with Thomas Weyhl, he sought the companionship of other deaf forty-niners, he had married a deaf woman, and he never wavered in his support for residential schools for deaf children. He was a risk taker and he welcomed debate, but he remained firm in his resistance to Flournoy's arguments. He had lived the life of a pioneer and his experiences were indeed lessons for those who harbored utopian dreams. Twenty-five years earlier, while he was a pupil at the Hartford school, Edmund wrote of the wisdom that comes through experience: "Self education is probably the best . . . for those who have learned by experience their own powers of mind will not readily submit to be led by others."[22]

The debate on the deaf state took place mostly through letters written over a three-year period.[23] During this exchange of letters, Edmund and Flournoy locked horns. Edmund agreed with little except giving women the right to vote if such a commonwealth were formed. "Mr. Flournoy belongs to [a] class of dreamers; and, like many of them, he, while tracing out his castle in the air, gives but superficial attention to the nature of the materials with which it is to be built, or the foundation on which it is to be laid." In his lengthy letter, Edmund argued that rather than having a convention of deaf people vote "to migrate to the West, to Oregon, to the South Sea Islands, or to the moon, I would suggest that they discuss the subject,—for thereby information may be diffused, reflection excited, and good done."[24]

Although some other deaf leaders supported Flournoy's idea, the artist and poet John Carlin ridiculed Flournoy profusely. The revered Laurent Clerc, after discussing the matter at the third meeting of the New England Gallaudet Association of Deaf-Mutes, summarized that there was a general consensus that the "present circumstances" of deaf people in society were preferred, and that Flournoy's proposal had too many practical difficulties.[25]

ॐ≶৫ॐ

THE education of deaf children changed radically in the latter half of the nineteenth century. Higher education became accessible for the first time and a controversy over how best to teach and communicate with deaf students erupted in the field. For the most part, Edmund stayed away from the methods controversy, but he took note of the changes and made his readers aware of them. The American Asylum in Hartford, as well as some of the other schools for deaf children, offered "high classes" to prepare deaf pupils for college-level work, but very few deaf students actually attended college. The communication barriers that prevented them from entering college suddenly disappeared in 1864 when Abraham Lincoln signed the Act of Incorporation creating the National Deaf-Mute College (now Gallaudet University), Washington, D.C. Edward Miner Gallaudet, the youngest son of Thomas Hopkins Gallaudet (founder of the American Asylum) became the first president of the new college. The college opened many doors for deaf men, and later women, to pursue careers in a variety of professions previously unavailable to them. In 1869, Edmund reprinted an article from the *Boston Advertiser* about the first graduation of the National Deaf-Mute College. The reporter marveled that one young graduate "delivered his oration in the sign language—speaking with such force and elegance and intonation, that, deaf as you were to his words, you could hardly help hearing many ideas."[26]

Edward Miner Gallaudet, like his father, was a staunch believer in the use of sign language to instruct deaf students. Until the mid-1860s, most teachers and administrators in the state schools for deaf children agreed with him. But then, an alternative method—the oral method—began to take hold, one that advocated the use of speech and lipreading to the exclusion of signs. In 1867 two new schools opened that employed the oral method, the New York Institution for the Improved Instruction of Deaf-Mutes in New York City, and the Clarke Institution for Deaf Mutes in Northampton, Massachusetts. Deaf education in the United States was forever changed.

In Europe, many of the schools for deaf children had already implemented the oral method. Edward Miner Gallaudet traveled through Europe in the spring of 1867 to see firsthand how the method was being used. When he returned, he addressed a meeting of the Conference of Principals of Institutions for the Deaf and urged the principals to offer speech training, or articulation classes, in their schools. He called for the creation of a "combined method" that would give students the benefit of both manual and oral methods. Within a year, the Iowa school was among those with an "oral teacher."[27]

Many of the school principals at the 1868 conference likely assumed that only a small percentage of their students would need articulation training. Certainly, few could have foreseen the impact that two oral schools would have on the established system of instruction in the country. However, within a few decades, more than seventy schools had shifted to oral-only instruction, and many deaf teachers had lost their jobs.

During this turmoil, Edmund focused his own energies on constructive discourse on education. In the mid-1870s he visited the Pennsylvania Institution, where he was shown a large mercantile ledger that was used to document daily lessons. He studied the lessons and then met with the teachers. One of the teachers was greatly impressed with "the gentle yet judicial manner in which he dissected them [the lessons] and showed us their blemishes, and the views he then expressed stamped him to us as a born teacher, one who, as editor of the Anamosa Eureka, had his light under a bushel, and one who, in a school for the deaf, could not have failed to have left a deep impress for good upon the work."[28]

At the national level, Edmund shared his perspectives with other educators in the *American Annals of the Deaf*. In 1877, he wrote an article titled "Miss Martineau and Deaf-Mutes." In this piece, he reminisced about his days as a teacher at the American Asylum in Hartford, during which the British writer Harriet Martineau, who had used an ear trumpet herself, described deaf people in a negative light. Edmund's article compared the education of deaf students then with the present, summarizing how much change had occurred in forty years. Deaf children in the 1830s had been limited to about four years of study, there was no high class or college (National Deaf-Mute College), no newspapers or journals, no clearly defined system of instruction in general acceptance. The focus then was on "charity" and this tended to lower the self-respect of deaf pupils. Over the years, Edmund conveyed to Lewis Weld his belief that the word "charity" should be discarded and that deaf children, as a matter of common justice, should be in school for more years. "Time passed," Edmund wrote, "and now the idea is in practice, and the improvement is very great. Forty years have accomplished what I hoped for, and the teachers of to-day may be certain that forty years hence will see still further advances."[29]

1879 was a particularly busy year for Edmund. He published an analysis of punctuation as an aid in the education of deaf children in the *American Annals of the Deaf;* he received mention and his portrait was included in a history of Jones County published by the Chicago Historical Society; and he launched Frank's career during a visit to the Iowa School for the Deaf in Council Bluffs. In a meeting with the superintendent, he learned that the school needed an instructor. He thought that Frank might be interested in considering the education of deaf children as his life's work, especially because Frank had been a mathematics teacher at Iowa State College for two years and was a fluent signer.

Frank began teaching at the Iowa School for the Deaf on December 1, 1879, after completing the term at Iowa State College. He first became aware of the oral method of instruction at the Iowa school, which had hired a teacher for articulation classes in 1869. The *American Annals of the Deaf* reported on Frank's new position at the Iowa school, commenting that he had arrived there "with the advantage of having been familiar with the language of signs from infancy."[30] The following year, the Iowa Legislature appropriated $1,000 to the Iowa school to be used for the purchase of a printing office. Frank became foreman of the printing office as well as editor of the *Deaf-Mute Hawk-Eye* (now the *Iowa Hawkeye*), in addition to his full-time job as a teacher. Given his experience in his father's printing business, Frank possessed "peculiar qualifications for this work." With knowledge of the trade gained from his father, he was considered ideal for this new venture.[31]

Frank stayed in Iowa until 1883, when he accepted a teaching position at the Pennsylvania Institution for the Deaf. By this time, schools for the deaf in the United States were undergoing a shift from manual or combined methods to oral instruction, especially with the younger children. The impetus for this shift was an international meeting of teachers and administrators in September 1880, in Milan, Italy. Of the 164 delegates to the meeting, only 5 were from the United States, and one of them was the lone deaf delegate. Most of the rest were from France and Italy, and they were strong supporters of the oral method. These delegates pushed for the following resolution, which passed with overwhelming support; only the Americans and one English teacher voted against it.[32]

The congress, considering the incontestable superiority of speech over signs, for restoring deaf-mutes to social life and for giving them greater facility in language, declares that the method of articulation should have preference over that of signs in the instruction and education of the deaf and dumb."[33]

The Pennsylvania school did not take long to adopt the oral philosophy. By 1883 it had divided into manual and oral departments. Frank Booth began teaching in the manual department. Within a few years, he was in charge of the Primary Manual Department, and soon after that, he became principal of the Advanced Manual Department. He added printing to the industrial education program and served as editor of the school's paper, *Our Little World*. As time passed, he became increasingly invested in the oral method.

When Frank Booth first arrived at the Pennsylvania Institution for the Deaf, the "oral" and "manual" students could interact outside of the classroom. Later, the school attempted to completely segregate these students. The principal of the school, Albert Louis Edgerton Crouter, was a committed oralist and a member of the Executive Committee of the American Association to Promote the Teaching of Speech to the Deaf (AAPTSD). Under Crouter's influence, Frank's allegiance to sign language changed. He switched departments and soon became head of the Intermediate Oral Department, where deaf children were taught exclusively through the use of speech and speechreading (lipreading). The Pennsylvania school's administrators reported better academic achievement among the students who received oral instruction, but they did not take into consideration that these students often had better hearing. Crouter, in particular, blamed lower achievement on the "injurious effect" of sign language. He went so far as to conclude that "when a deaf child cannot be educated by the application of proper oral methods, it is useless to hope for any marked success under any method."[34]

Frank knew better. Both of his parents were well educated, and both had received their education through sign language. All three of the Booth children could sign and they occasionally interpreted for their parents. Hattie recognized and appreciated the influence her father's great intellect had on her own development.

> For years every night after father had read the papers, he would tell mother the news and would generally discuss it at length. I was always interested listener in, and my opinions concerning public matters were naturally

Frank Booth rose quickly in the ranks of oral advocates. He is pictured here *(back row, 4th from left)* at the 1894 meeting of the American Association for the Promotion of Teaching Speech to the Deaf. Alexander Graham Bell is standing on Booth's left, and on Bell's left is Frank's superintendent, A.L.E. Crouter. Edward Miner Gallaudet is seated in the front row *(4th from the right)*. Courtesy of Gallaudet University Archives.

formed according to father's views. I have noticed since that I am more interested in public affairs than the average woman, and I attribute it to my early training by father.[35]

⁂

FRANK Booth's rise in the ranks of oralist educators stands in strange juxtaposition to his father's emergence as a leading voice in the American Deaf community. Edmund's role in the "war of methods" raging among educators of deaf students was primarily as a patriarchal chief of the signing Deaf community. His meaningful contributions in both the deaf and hearing worlds were publicly recognized several times in 1880. On May 5, the National Deaf-Mute College awarded him an honorary degree. Alexander Graham Bell, the inventor of the telephone as well as a leading proponent of the oral method, delivered one of the graduation speeches. He talked about the Visible Speech system, a method of teaching articulation that his father, Melville Bell, had created. The commencement speaker was the Honorable J. Randolph Tucker, a member of Congress from Virginia. Following these presentations, Edmund received the degree of Master of Arts, in recognition of his attainments as a scholar and as a journalist.[36]

Three months later, Edmund traveled to Cincinnati, Ohio, for a meeting that resulted in the formation of the National Association of the Deaf (NAD). Members of the Deaf community had begun planning the meeting a year earlier in reaction to what they saw as the oppressive strategies of the hearing administrators in the schools. The planners included Edwin Allan Hodgson of New York, Robert P. McGregor of Ohio, and "mighty men of valor" such as "the gigantic Edmund Booth, Dudley Webster George and others." The convention opened on August 25, 1880, and lasted three days. George Veditz, a two-time president of the NAD, characterized this remarkable assembly as

> the FIRST great meeting of the class to be absolutely independent of leading strings held in other hands than their own. No superintendent or principal, no hearing teacher, had anything to do either with [this] program or arrangements. It was even regarded as unnecessary to provide interpreters. The members came, some from long distances, and instead of camping at some school, paid their hotel and transportation bills and possessed a new sense of independence, well-being and importance and of sufficiency unto themselves.[37]

The official title of the Cincinnati convention was "National Convention of Deaf-Mutes," reflecting perhaps the parlance of the time, as well as the delegates' opposition to the oral method. Veditz noted in his history of the founding of the NAD that "in Cincinnati the designations *mutes* and *deaf-mutes* were freely used by superb speakers and lip-readers like Booth, Hodgson and McGregor, though even then speech and lip-reading were taught in all our schools."[38]

After the opening prayer on the first day of the convention, Robert P. McGregor nominated Edmund Booth as temporary chairman, and the 81 deaf men and women present approved the nomination by acclamation. Selah Wait of Illinois and Henry C. Ryder of New York, who was editor of the *Deaf Mutes Journal,* escorted Edmund to the chair. He was a formidable presence, still "tall and muscular, with hair and beard as white as drifted snow. . . . His step was then strong, his form erect, his intellect alert, and his demeanor one of dignified enthusiasm. He was then in his seventieth year."[39]

The first convention of the National Association of the Deaf was held in Cincinnati, Ohio, in 1880. Edmund Booth presided as Temporary Chairman. Booth was called the "Honored Nestor" of the American Deaf community, in reference to the poet Homer's wise and aged counselor. Courtesy of Gallaudet University Archives.

> On taking the chair, he delivered an interesting speech, thanking the Convention for the honor. In the course of his remarks, he called attention to the wonderful change for the better that had taken place in the intellectual and social status of the deaf-mutes since he left school, over forty years ago. He said the large number of intelligent faces he was confronted with, was proof of the value of education. His remarks were vigorously applauded.[40]

On the third day of the convention, the delegates discussed several religious denominations and their involvement in the spiritual welfare of deaf people. Edmund then addressed the convention on the need for more accessible church services. He was obviously irritated at a recent experience in church and took the opportunity to speak up for the rights of deaf people in that regard. He mentioned having attended an Episcopal service in 1877 in Chicago, where "the windows admitted the clear light of heaven. It all went well and was perfectly satisfactory." However, some weeks later, he attended church again in Chicago and "a dim religious light" prevailed, a "flat reversal of the command, 'Let there be light.'" He continued:

Two evenings ago, some of us attended Episcopal service at one of the churches in this city of Cincinnati. There were three clergymen for the mutes and one for the hearing. . . . in large degree, a farce. It is hard language, I know, and I speak it not willingly, but it is time to tell them the plain truth, for not one of the three seems to have given thought to the fact that to bring light to the mind of a deaf-mute, there must be light for the eye.[41]

Edmund complained that the gaslights in the church were arranged solely for the hearing congregation and that the wide, white sleeves of the clergymen's robes fluttered as they signed, making it nearly impossible to understand what was being preached. "Our preachers should have something of that most uncommon of all things, common sense," Edmund told the audience. "Thomas H. Gallaudet, who first established preaching by signs, was largely possessed of that commodity, and would never have dreamed of preaching to mutes in a darkened church or with lights so placed as to dazzle the eyes and throw little or no light where light is most needed."[42]

Edmund's topic was not out of place at this convention. The general theme of the meeting was the self-advocacy role that a national organization of deaf people could fill. By banding together, educated deaf people would have a stronger voice in society and would gain more control over their own destiny. Theodore A. Froehlich, one of the New York delegates, typified this attitude in his presentation, "Importance of Association among MUTES for Mutual Improvement."[43] Once the delegates voted to establish the NAD, they nominated Edmund as its first president, an honor he declined because of his age. Looking back, Veditz commented that Edmund's role in the early years of the NAD's formation was more than appropriate. Edmund "was the first successful deaf-mute publisher. His paper, the Anamosa *Eureka*, was for years the official publication of Jones County, Iowa. . . . Booth, always eight years older than the Hartford school, was beyond doubt the greatest American deaf-mute of his generation."[44]

Ironically, there was little discussion at the first NAD convention on the subject of oralism, even though the Milan Congress was scheduled to convene just one month later. According to Veditz, "the first definite instance of revolt of the adult American deaf against the dictates of the German-Bell propaganda" occurred three years later, at the Second National Convention of Deaf-Mutes in New York City. "The adult deaf were definitely pledged to the proposition that they were entitled to opinions and the expression of these opinions on all matters affecting the class, educational, most of all."[45]

≈§?≈

FOLLOWING the Gallaudet graduation and the NAD convention, Edmund visited several residential schools for deaf children in the eastern states as well as those in Iowa and Nebraska. "Having been, half a century ago, a pupil at Hartford, and afterwards a teacher, I felt a natural curiosity to ascertain whether any, and, if so, what changes had taken place in the method and manner of instruction during the forty years that have passed since I retired from the profession," he wrote in the *Annals*. Edmund reported that the signs were "nearly the same" as those used half a century earlier. "We still adhere to the old sign for President, from Monroe's three-cornered hat, and for Governor we designate the cockade worn by the dignitary on grand occasions three generations ago."[46] But on the subject of instructional methods, Edmund did not hesitate to express his disappointment.

> The late Harvey P. Peet, in an article in the *Annals*, insisted that "language is a science," but, in my recent visit to the various institutions, I found the books and the methods in the younger classes presenting a process which might properly be called *memorizing chaos*. Of the older classes I do not speak here, but I could not avoid feeling that a great amount of valuable time is thrown away for want of a few grains of common sense in those who prepare the printed books for the younger pupils. . . . It is forgotten that unlike the parrot, the pupil in most cases has the faculty of thinking—that is, analyzing, comparing, combining, etc—even if the teacher has not. The sooner these qualities are brought into play in connection with verbal memory, the better, for then the pupils would not only memorize, but would also understand, and this in itself adds to the pleasure of study. It brings

into action a variety of mental faculties of verbal memory, and in some cases the latter is the weakest or most defective of all.[47]

Edmund's hectic schedule in 1880 left him both tired and inspired. He had renewed many acquaintances and he returned home knowing that his own pen remained as trenchant as a sword. He had observed a new generation of deaf people who would stand upon his tall shoulders and courageously take the platform to fight for the rights of deaf people to participate in making decisions that would affect their own future. His own work, however, was far from finished. In 1881, he and four other deaf men met in Des Moines and organized the Iowa Association of the Deaf. He also became that organization's "guiding spirit."[48] In September 1884, at the Second Convention of Iowa Deaf-Mutes in Cedar Rapids, eighty deaf persons elected Edmund president for the ensuing year.

ॐ۞ॐ

FRANK Booth's pursuit of oralism in no way estranged him from his signing deaf parents. No evidence can be found that Edmund, in particular, argued with his son over this stance. Perhaps Edmund did not wish to interfere with Frank's professional life. In every other regard, Frank was a very loving son who kept his parents informed of his work, his family, and his travels. He set aside a writing hour, usually on Sundays, to correspond with Edmund and Mary Ann. He wrote nearly every week to his parents. In January 1885 he told them about his proposal for a student evaluation system that would give language skills a higher weight than arithmetic, history, and geography. He also wrote, "should the [superintendent position] of the Iowa Inst. be offered me, I should feel it a compliment. But as for accepting it I might or might not."[49]

Frank made it clear to his parents that he did not support the use of sign language as a method of communication with young deaf children. He noted a gradual "improvement" in the oral method and in student achievement; he was not discouraged by slow improvement because he believed that "changes may not be made rapidly to be effectual and permanent.[50]

Certainly, it is a great mystery why Edmund did not at least mention private arguments with Frank over communication and educational philosophies. The oralist movement, which ultimately encouraged deaf people to live in the "hearing" world, represented the antithesis of the Deaf community in which Edmund and Mary Ann lived. On issues such as slavery, the rights of women, temperance, and the value of the family, the Booths all agreed. It appears that this latter issue—family loyalty—was a dominating influence that muted Edmund's opinions on oralism and caused him to keep them to his innermost thoughts.

TWELVE

The Sound of Trumpets

❧❦❧❦

THE voluminous correspondence between Edmund and Frank while Frank was in Philadelphia indicates that Edmund and Mary Ann spent the final two decades of their lives enjoying their expanding family. Between 1876 and 1890, Hattie and Reverend George LeClere had seven children. Frank, who married Marion Elizabeth Hendershot in 1892, had three children.[1]

Hattie and George LeClere spent a total of thirteen years in Iowa, Wisconsin, and South Dakota before they moved to a ranch in Hardeman County in northwest Texas. In the fall of 1888, while George prepared their new house, Hattie and the children, ranging in age from 2 to 12, went to visit Edmund and Mary Ann in Anamosa. In November, the family left at 4 AM by stage to board a train for home. Hattie received a letter from her father soon after she arrived in Texas.

> He wrote that the night following the day I left he could not sleep for thinking of the journey I was taking with the children. He said he went to bed, but got up again, dressed and sat up the rest of the night. I had expected mother to worry, but had not thought of father doing so. He was always so optimistic and philosophical and never wasted much time in worrying. So his failure to sleep gave me an insight into his nature I had never had before, and I loved him as I had never loved him before.[2]

Between 1885 and 1898, Edmund worked on writing his autobiography, something his children had been urging him to do. He found this task difficult for several reasons—first because he did not wish to focus on his own life, and second because he suffered from numerous ailments that

The Booth family: *left to right,* Edmund Booth, Thomas Eyre Booth, Harriet "Hattie" Booth LeClere, Frank Walworth Booth, and Mary Ann Walworth Booth. From the Booth family album, courtesy of The Haggin Museum, Stockton, California.

prevented him from writing more than a few paragraphs at a sitting. Mary Ann was not well either. She had never fully recovered from a bout of influenza, and she was not able to perform housework except in a slow manner. Edmund devoted much of his time to taking care of her. They hired a young woman one summer to help them, but she left in January because of ill health. Edmund and Mary Ann then moved into Thomas's house a short distance away on Ford Street. Only their lawns and an alley separated the two houses.

Edmund's personality still drew people, young and old, to him. His love for nature never dwindled. He was always concerned that the wild birds would be disturbed and he made sure that both food and water were provided for them. As one friend wrote,

Everyone spoke of him as Grandpa Booth, and the little children in the neighborhood who could communicate with him did not hesitate to ask any favor at his hands, which usually consisted of permission to play in the yard, or pluck the fruits or flowers that grew in such abundance by his door. . . . at one time, a meadow mole, so destructive to beautiful lawns, was caught in a neighboring yard and not much injured. It was placed in an old tin vessel and was shown to the little children as a curiosity, Grandson Edmund Booth among them. When Grandpa saw it he said, "Let it go in my yard—plenty of room—they do no harm. In his estimation, every living thing had the right to life, liberty, and the pursuit of happiness in its own way.[3]

Edmund was a teacher throughout his life. The neighborhood children brought him ice cream and lemonade and, sometimes, flowers, both wild and cultivated. He always asked them the names of the plants.

Edmund and Mary Ann celebrated their golden anniversary in July 1890. On this occasion, they received a letter from Mary Ann's brother James in South Boston. "I understand that your friends are about to celebrate the fiftieth anniversary of your marriage," he wrote, "but how the sleeping memories of the distant past are awakened by an event of this kind." He was carried back not only 50 years, but into their early childhood.

I think of you now—Mary Ann—as I saw you when, at two or three years of age, a beautiful golden haired child. You got lost in the thickly wooded swamp near our old home in Canaan. I wonder if you remember it. You had been missed for some time when the family began to be alarmed, and commenced a hunt for you. I suspected that you might have wandered away into this little forest and began a search in that direction. At length I spied the little wanderer, with a little net on her head, to prevent the wanton wind from playing too freely with her curls, trudging along towards home, having got within sight of the house, and before she had discovered me, I heard her repeating to herself—"I glad I got the way. I glad I got the way," and we both went home rejoicing.[4]

James also remembered when the Congregational minister of Canaan made a pastoral call at the Walworth house. "Father, who was always very proud of you, in order to show off his smart baby daughter, took you up on his knee and had you read a chapter in the family bible: this was of course before you were four years old. For, as I understand, your deafness came on at about that age." James recalled how at a public exhibition Mary Ann was lifted up onto a platform, where she recited a poem. "At the risk of being suspected of flattering you," James wrote, "which I fancy would not spoil you at this distance from your girlhood, I will say that we used to think you the prettiest girl in the town, and without intending any disparagement of your sisters, 'the flower of the family.' "[5]

James told Mary Ann that he still possessed a stack of letters written by their mother, Philura Walworth, and he quoted from one sent from Bond County, Illinois, in 1845. She spoke of missing Thomas after Mary Ann had returned to Iowa, and she described how he would reach up his little hand to help his grandparents up the cellar stairs, try to help carry in the pail of milk, and "many such little acts of kindness he was always ready to do, which doubly endeared him to us."[6] Thomas was only 3 years old at the time, and his "help" was more lovable than practical. Philura also wrote,

> I sometimes fear you will set your heart too much upon him. If you do, he may be taken from you, or live only to be a grief to you. But I hope and desire that he will live to be a great blessing, and make suitable return of love to you for all your tender care and love for him. My dear Mary Ann, I cannot help looking back at the time when you was [sic] of the tender age of your little son—a lovely and well beloved little daughter.[7]

Thomas did grow up as his grandmother had hoped, although she did not live to see this. In the years that followed Edmund and Mary Ann's golden anniversary, in particular, Thomas and Gertrude were always nearby to assist his aging parents. They were with Edmund and Mary Ann during many touching moments. One day Gertrude saw Mary Ann look up from her bed and call Edmund's attention to some beautiful lily blossoms outside the opened south window of the house. Mary Ann fingerspelled, "Behold the lilies of the field," and Edmund, seizing the quotation from the Scriptures, responded with, "They toil not, neither do they spin, yet I say unto you that Solomon in all his glory was not arrayed like one of these." Edmund smiled at his wife in gratitude, remembering that he had learned these words at his mother's knee nearly 90 years ago.[8]

Edmund and Mary Ann Walworth Booth celebrated their golden wedding anniversary on July 26, 1890. Their sons, Frank *(left)* and Thomas *(right)*, were in Anamosa for this occasion, but their daughter Harriet was unable to attend. She lived in Texas and had recently given birth to her seventh child. Courtesy of Helen Heckenlaible and Wilma Spice.

Frank wrote weekly to his parents from Philadelphia. He told them about activities at the school, his correspondence with Hattie, and his courtship of Marion Elizabeth Hendershot, who had been a teacher at the Michigan School for the Deaf in Flint. Frank and Marion married in August 1892. Frank discussed politics with his parents, expressing hope that the Republicans would win the election in November. He described a football game between Pennsylvania and Princeton that attracted 18,000 people who saw Pennsylvania win for the first time in 18 years. In March 1893 he described the Pennsylvania Institution's new campus in the Mt. Airy district of Philadelphia. Frank edited a journal, *The Silent Educator*, and published it with Samuel G. Davidson, a deaf colleague who had formerly edited *The Silent World*. He sent copies to his father, and when Edmund did not respond, Frank admonished him, "You have not written what you thought of the paper."[9] Frank also encouraged his mother to write.

At times Frank tired of his work and sought support from his parents. In 1893 he told his parents that both he and his wife Marion wished for other work and other responsibilities: "It is no great fun to be at the head of a family of 175 people, mostly children!"[10] At the same time, Frank encouraged his father to stay active in education, "to write something upon an educational topic . . . in the *Educator* or the *Annals*. It would be well received, anything you might say, as from the oldest living teacher in America."[11] Edmund did remain active. In 1895, at the age of 85, he attended the World Congress of the Deaf in Chicago, and he met with George Veditz, the champion of sign language.

In May 1895 Mary Ann received a visit from her brother James. "It seemed good to be with you so long," he wrote to her upon returning home. He wished they lived nearer so they could see each other more often, and he told her he hoped her new medicine did her "lots of good."[12]

Frank too, was growing increasingly concerned about his mother's health. In one letter, he tried to comfort his parents with news about their grandson Edmund, who, he reported, "looks like his grandfather."[13] He sent them photographs and a list of twenty words young Edmund had learned to speak. At the end of his March 1, 1897, letter, Frank wrote, "I know it is hard for mother to write now, but we like to hear from her that much the more."[14] His letter of October 18, 1897, ended with the short note, "I feel anxious about mother."[15]

Mary Ann had always cherished her independence. After all, she had spent nearly 58 years on the frontier wilderness. As she lost strength in her final years, she was angered at her inability to perform household duties. Confined to her bed, she was no longer able to attend church. She weakened gradually over a period of several years. Edmund stayed with Mary Ann daily; their children and grandchildren visited them when possible. On January 18, 1898, when Hattie left to return to her home in Texas, Mary Ann, sensing her time was short, slowly spelled out on failing fingers, H-E-A-V-E-N! She seemed curious as to why she was allowed to linger on for so long in her weakened state. She wanted to let go.

Mary Ann Walworth Booth died on Sunday, January 25, 1898, at 11:30 PM. She was 80 years, 11 months, and 2 days old. Her funeral was held on Tuesday, January 27, at 2 PM at the First Congregational Church in Anamosa. The Rev. S. F. Millikan gave the funeral eulogy, "The Heroic Life." He related that Edmund was once Mary Ann's Classics teacher. He traced the Walworth family journey from New Hampshire to Illinois and then to Iowa, where they located on the Buffalo Forks and erected saw mills and flour mills. He told of Edmund's arrival thereafter and their marriage on July 26, 1840.

Reverend Millikan also commented on Mary Ann's character, noting that "she husbanded his [Edmund's] earnings in the mines with wise, constant and judicious care and made investment that gave homes not only to the two families and this church but to all others residing in this block." He praised "her clear discernment in all business matters and her industry and executive force [which] were very marked for one measurably isolated by infirmity." As a mother, Mary Ann "sought by example and training to prepare her children well for their work in life, remembering steadily and lovingly the supreme fact that integrity of character, purity, and steadfast faith in God constitute the strongest and safest foundations." Even though she had never heard her husband's or her children's voices, "she lived that her children rise up and call her blessed." Millikan closed by saying "it is easy to say our sister was shut out from social ambitions by infirmity, but it is also easy to see that she would not have yielded to their seductions or followed their false lights had it been otherwise. She had learned that duty doing is the gateway to nobility; that duty doing is earthly as well as heavenly glory."[16]

Mary Ann was one of the founders of Anamosa's Congregational Church, which was organized in 1846, and she had been an active member for over 51 years. She regularly attended services even though she could not hear the Gospel or choir. She told her children and grandchildren many times how much she longed to hear a sermon and to hear the music and singing.

Frank was in Philadelphia when his mother died, and, therefore, was unable to attend the funeral. In a letter to Edmund, he wrote that he knew Mary Ann wanted an end to her suffering. "My sorrow is for you, left alone. . . . Companionship for nearly fifty-eight years, almost uninterrupted, means dependence upon it as a part of our nature, and loss of it is loss of part of life itself."[17]

Harriet had just returned to Texas, so she, too, missed the funeral. She wrote that even though she was unprepared for her mother's death, she also knew that her mother wanted the end to come. "How I wish I could have been with her to the last," she wrote in a letter to her father.[18] Harriet later reminisced,

Mother was of a social nature. She enjoyed people. She was cut off by her infirmity from the intercourse with people which her nature craved. As I grow older I realize and understand better her isolation. If only I could have understood when she was with us, I could have and would have done more to make her life brighter and more cheery.[19]

Mary Ann Walworth was buried in the family plot in Riverside Cemetery in Anamosa. Reverend Millikan consoled Edmund through pad and pencil, expressing heartfelt appreciation of Mary Ann's worth and of Edmund's great loss. Edmund read the written words slowly. "This is the hardest blow that ever struck me," he replied. Then, raising his right hand, he spoke two words to the minister, though there were tears in his eyes, "Storms Strengthen."[20]

After Mary Ann died, Edmund lived alone in his one-story brick house, his only companion a black cat. Thomas's family brought him daily meals. Thomas, Hattie, and Frank continued to encourage Edmund to complete his autobiography. The pain in his hands, however, was disabling, which lead him to read about scrivener's palsy, or writer's cramp. Edmund did force himself to return to the writing, though, because he sensed it was "time to finish this long story of one's life."[21]

On March 13, 1893, he wrote the following very touching letter to Frank and Marion:

> My dear children—
> Since mother died I have no heart for writing letters and have answered

After Mary Ann's death, Thomas and Gertrude took care of Edmund. This photograph, taken on April 8, 1901, shows four generations of the Booth family: Edmund *(far left)*, Thomas *(far right)*, Thomas's daughter Mabel Gertrude Booth Brewer *(center)*, and Mabel's daughter Gertrude Delavan Brewer *(on Mabel's lap)*. Courtesy of Helen Heckenlaible and Wilma Spice.

only two out of near a dozen or so. After fifty seven years of a trusting and agreeable home life a break up is no trifle. Many a time I have sat and dozed in my chair, waked suddenly and looked around for her to help her if help was wanted. I have been doing this for more than a year, and now she is gone. It is hard to realize. It is about seven weeks since she died and I have not been in the street more than once. . . . I am very well satisfied to live in my own house and no bother from any body, but it is so lonely without the presence of Mother & will endure it to the end. With books and especially the daily papers I can forget for a while what has been. I will not need to wait long. I can easily imagine Mother as being with the child of 17 months [the first Harriet] for whom she mourned so much, and now she enjoys a reunion never to be broken.

Love to you all,

Father[22]

Until his final days as editor of the *Anamosa Eureka*, Edmund remained a strong advocate of quality education for deaf children. In 1898, when the Iowa School for the Deaf cut the salary of its most prominent teacher by more than one-half and lowered the salaries of other teachers, Edmund used the *Eureka* to argue in their favor. He predicted that the best teachers would leave for better-paying jobs and the deaf children would suffer.

Days turned to weeks and weeks to months as Edmund adjusted to a life without Mary Ann. He retired as editor of the *Eureka* after more than 40 years at its helm. The standards and policies of the *Eureka* were for decades the personal standards and policies of the Booth family. Many years later, the editors of the *Eureka* lauded Edmund's

Staunch loyalty to the republican party, hatred of disunion, hatred of the liquor business and the use of liquor, loyalty to the church and its standards, loyalty to education, and to all upbuilding influences, loyalty to everything that meant the development and growth of Anamosa and Jones County, but above all a personal and sympathetic interest in [Edmund Booth's] friends and neighbors as individuals, as he recorded with joy the family good news, or recorded tenderly their sorrows and bereavements. His interests followed his old friends to distant communities, or recalled their virtues and good deeds after their memories had begun to fade. And in their turn they came back to him in his later years with good wishes and kindly words of appreciation.[23]

Thomas and Gertrude took care of Edmund on a daily basis after Mary Ann died. In 1901, their daughter Bertha became ill, and the doctors advised them to take her to Colorado for a while. Frank and Thomas arranged for Edmund to stay with Frank for the summer. Thomas assumed that his father would be enthusiastic about observing the classes and teaching methods at the Pennsylvania Institution for the Deaf.

> I supposed we were all in substantial accord in that respect, including father himself. But what a mistake! Father, to all appearances busy with pleasant anticipations, suddenly burst out: "It is no trifling matter for me to leave my home; and if the ticket had not been bought I would remain here." His voice shook with deep emotion and I thought he was going to break down entirely. It was a complete revelation to me, and I think to all the rest; but this new view gave me a realization of Father's loneliness without mother and the old home that I never had before.[24]

Edmund may have thought the move to Philadelphia was permanent, so Thomas reassured him it was only for the summer. Although almost 91 and feeble, he agreed to go. This trip marked another turning point in Edmund's life in terms of his legacy in the Deaf community. While in Philadelphia, he accepted an invitation to address the Clerc Literary Association. He was probably the oldest living pioneer educator of deaf persons in the United States who could boast of having personally known Laurent Clerc and Thomas Hopkins Gallaudet.

On Thursday evening, May 2, 1901, Edmund addressed a crowd of 100 deaf people. He paid a moving tribute to Thomas H. Gallaudet, and he showed great excitement when he spoke of Laurent Clerc, who had taught him longest. Having outlived his teacher by many years, Edmund proudly counseled the audience in Clerc's tradition, encouraging them to cultivate the virtue of integrity as an indispensable ingredient of success. Following this presentation, Frank gave a short address, expressing pleasure that his Philadelphia friends had the opportunity to meet his father.

Edmund Booth remained active after he retired from publishing the *Anamosa Eureka*. One of his last public appearances was at the Laurent Clerc Literary Association meeting in Philadelphia in 1901. Courtesy of Gallaudet University Archives.

The Silent Worker, the popular periodical of the American Deaf community, reported on Edmund's speech and extolled his many achievements.

> Father time is very generous to Mr. Booth, if we may regard longevity of life a blessing, for few attain his age of fourscore years and nigh eleven, and,

barring accident, he appears to have a number of years to spare. Tall and big as he is, with his spruce white beard and clean, well-preserved round features which are so suggestive of good health, he has a patriarchal appearance that is as interesting as it is admirable. Of all the deaf whom the writer has seen anywhere, some only approach in stature while none impressed him with as much interest as Mr. Booth has. . . . A man who has done life's duty well, who has made his mark in his chosen calling, who has reflected so much honor upon his class, as we know Mr. Booth to have done, ought, we believe, to be given the satisfaction of knowing before the grave closes over him that the world appreciates his life labors.[25]

Edmund returned to Anamosa, just as Thomas had promised, and there he spent his remaining years. He stayed home most of the time and read as much as he could. When the vision in his good eye began to fail, he seemed to take it in stride; he had made one eye do the work of two ears and two eyes for most of his life, and he felt that it was nearly time to give it a rest.

Edmund's once vigorous gait slowed considerably in the early 1900s. Thomas, who had once had difficulty keeping up with his father during their walks together, fondly remembered how his father's broad shoulders always came to his rescue. "A sign from me was all that was needed. Down he went and I clambered on. The comfort, the restful feeling that came to me so many times I never will forget." Now, as he provided loving care to his father, he found more comfort, knowing that "perhaps in [these] after years the burden-bearing was reversed in a sense, and just as satisfying to us both."[26]

Edmund had much time to reminisce and finish his autobiography. He often thought about his beloved Mary Ann. One night he dreamed of her and their daughter who had died in infancy. In this dream, the first Harriet had grown to maturity and greeted him in afterlife. The last words he wrote in his autobiography were reflections on Mary Ann's death. He quoted from the Roman poet Festus: "She said she wished to die and so she died; There was no discord. It was music ceased."[27]

Thomas and Edmund spent many nights recalling events from long ago. On one such night, Thomas spelled out on his fingers to Edmund,

"God has been very good to you all these years." His father's response astonished him—Edmund exclaimed, " 'Oh, yes, yes,' and his voice broke, his frame quivered, and tears filled his eyes. The long reserve was broken at last. Thus suddenly was I overwhelmed."[28]

Although friends and relatives visited Edmund in his final years, he was largely isolated from the Deaf community. His last deaf visitor was the wife of George W. Veditz. During their time together, Edmund "did complain to her and spoke of his loneliness and of his happiness to meet once more a deaf [person] using the sign-language and handicapped as he was himself, before the final summons came."[29]

ॐ§ह

IN 1903, the 5 acres of land Mary Ann bought in 1851 for $90 and Edmund later donated (with about 48 feet of frontage) to the Congregational Society for a church, sold for $4,000. The Society used these funds for a new church on the corner of Booth and First streets. Mary Ann's prediction that the land would one day be valuable had proven true. Thomas later recognized his parents' contribution to Anamosa.

This five acre tract of brush, grass, scrub oaks and scattering forest trees, with a big pond and sometimes two or three, became the most important public block in Anamosa, with its post-office in place of the old church, its opera house, Eureka printing office, city hall, fire department, American Legion hall, public library building and business blocks and residences. That $90 that father dug out of California soil by hard knocks, mother, by the most rigid economy and good judgment saved for wise investment, made choice of this five acres way out on the military road . . . and the results of that choice have followed with corresponding benefits to the Booth family ever since, to say nothing of the Congregational church.[30]

In August 1904, the *Monticello Express* celebrated "Father Booth's" 94th birthday. "It is a delight to honor the achievements of such a man, and a pleasure to congratulate him upon the attainment of so advanced an age, full of honor, and blessed with the memory of things done."[31]

EDMUND Booth died on March 24, 1905, in Anamosa at the age of 94. He had been mentally alert until the last few weeks of his life, even though his physical health had declined. Frank arrived from Philadelphia three hours before his father died. The family said prayers at Thomas's house just before Edmund died. The Reverend A. O. Stevens preached the funeral sermon to a large gathering of friends and family members. He spoke of Edmund's teaching career, his work at the flour mill with the Walworths, and his stewardship of the *Anamosa Eureka*. Readings included the eleventh chapter of Matthew, one of the last selections of Scripture Edmund had read.[32]

No greater tribute could be paid to any man than the large number of friends and neighbors who assembled to pay their last respects. During the hour of Edmund Booth's funeral, all of the stores and businesses in Anamosa closed, and the district court, then in regular session, adjourned to allow the judge and attorneys to attend the funeral. Milton Remley, a former Iowa Attorney General, sent his condolences to Thomas: "Too often young men with no disability imagine that they cannot do anything worthwhile in life, and hence do not attempt it. I have admired your father's character and his earnestness in grasping the affairs of life and battling so successfully therewith. . . . The world is better for your father having lived. He did much to give tone and sentiment to the early days of Iowa history; and in the fullness of years he has passed to his reward."[33]

The following poem is one of the many tributes paid to Edmund Booth. John N. Davidson, a former printer with the *Eureka* who became a minister, penned the poem in memory of his friend and mailed it to Thomas.

Ninety Years of Silence

His mother's songs he heard; then silence fell.
To him all noiseless was his schoolmates' play
And birds with songs unheard filled all the day.
"Sad, sad," men sighed, "that he apart must dwell
As in a voiceless world." But let his life's work tell
How strong the resolute soul; how mighty they

Who beat beneath their feet the fears that sway
The timid and the weak. A proud farewell
We speak, for thou hast stood life's testing pain.
Thou wast the conqueror of thine adverse fate,
Sight of the soul, far reaching, thou didst gain;
Cry of the wronged made thee articulate:
Rights of the dumb thou didst with might maintain;
Deeds like thy Lord's: these we commemorate.[34]

Edmund Booth was the Deaf community's oldest representative, a man of wisdom who guided many others toward control of their own destiny. At the Convention of American Instructors of the Deaf held in North Carolina in July 1905, the nation's teachers noted that "besides his voluminous editorial writings, he contributed a number of articles to the *American Annals of the Deaf*, as well as to other publications principally historical. With the rest he was a poet, and poems that he wrote show beauty and loftiness of thought that are perhaps the best index of his character that remains to us."[35]

Edmund was also the newspaper fraternity's oldest member, the pioneer editor who pursued high ideals throughout his lifetime. He waged a vigorous campaign in the columns of his paper and wielded widespread influence. Many of the Iowa newspapers published tributes to him. The *Central City News Letter* summarized his life as "a complete success, using that word in its best sense. A pioneer journalist, a clever writer, a good citizen, a model parent and an industrious man, his life must indeed have been much more than an ordinarily successful one." The *Marion Register* praised him as "one of the best men in the state and country," and the *Iowa Register-Tribune* of Akron stated that "though Mr. Booth has done well, his departure needs not be accompanied by the sound of a trumpet. His life-long work speaks for itself. Peace to his ashes." The *Anamosa Eureka* said simply, "God's finger touched him and he slept."[36]

Afterword

❧❦❧

EARLY in March 2003, I sifted through the stacks of notes and photocopied pages that littered my study, searching for a way to capture the breadth of Edmund Booth's life in a few words. I found a letter from C. S. Millard, Edmund's former neighbor, that was published in the *Anamosa Eureka* after Edmund's death in 1905. The following passage summarizes well what I was looking for:

> And now he has gone, and what a rich inheritance has he left for his children, and to mankind. All men aim to leave something valuable on departing this life, the difference being in the thing itself. Money perishes. Fame is vouchsafed to but few—in most instances at best is soon dimmed by the finger of time, but the recollections of kind and gentle manners, ever living desires to accomplish great good; thoughtfulness of children which, in the raising of a family, affords such a rich opportunity for the development of a sweet and loving nature, had full play in the life of Grandpa Booth, and his children and children's children to the remotest generation can always refer to their ancestor with just pride and commendable satisfaction.[1]

That prophetic statement indeed became true. The Booth descendants have proudly cherished their heritage, preserving precious accounts of the lives of Edmund and Mary Ann. Their great-granddaughter, Helen Heckenlaible, was 97 years old when I began the research for this book. Edmund and Mary Ann's great-great-granddaughter, Wilma Spice, has worked for years with historians, librarians, curators, and others to bring the intriguing tale of the Booth family to life again. Wilma was the person who encouraged me to write this book. She knew I was deaf, loved history, and enjoyed writing about deaf people who *made* history. Never in all my prior book-writing adventures have I experienced such an enthusiastic group as the Booth descendants and their friends, who established an e-mail network and followed the progress of the book for two years. From my perspective as an educator of deaf students, the family's knowledge of their ancestors' lives underscores Edmund and Mary Ann Booth's belief in the value of connectedness.

While conducting research for this book, I found numerous other deaf miners and emigrants to California around the time Edmund was there. Benjamin Clough accompanied him across the Plains. Oliver Badger and Albert Barnard of Massachusetts, and Elisha Osgood of Maine, all of whom attended the American Asylum in Hartford (now known as the American School for the Deaf), went to California. There is a letter from another student from that school, Samuel Rowe, written on February 13, 1849, in which he expresses concern for the "unfortunate adventurers," Messrs. Mann and Dennison, "deafmutes both," who had also gone to California to seek gold. They were expected to return in several years, if they could avoid being "stabbed in such a dangerous enterprise."[2] In a letter to Edmund, Mary Ann mentions a deaf man named John Handy who took his family from Iowa to the gold mines. And in his final days in California, Edmund worked at Camp Seco with a deaf man named Herbert Weyhl, who "was wholly uneducated but a smart fellow and a good worker."[3] Other deaf emigrants to California included two of Weyhl's earlier mining partners who had been pupils at the Pennsylvania Institution in Philadelphia. They were so taken by the Australian gold stories that they left for that country. Other deaf people who came to California in the 1850s included William Neeley of Pennsylvania, a man named Hanser of Illinois, John Larue of New York, Samuel Clayton of Illinois, H. B. Crandall of New York, Benjamin Brazallair of Connecticut, and Mr. and Mrs. Glass of Ohio. Although some of these deaf individuals may have mined more gold than Edmund Booth, it was Edmund who was ultimately rich because he was literate and he left a fascinating paper trail that allows us

Edmund and Mary Ann's descendants, taken in 1912, in Anamosa, Iowa. *Standing left to right:* Gertrude Delavan Booth, Mabel Gertrude Booth Brewer, Gertrude Delavan Brewer, Helen Adele Brewer (later Heckenlaible), George Frederick LeClere, Marion Frances Booth; Robert Plues Booth, Marion Elizabeth Hendershot Booth, Edmund Hendershot Booth. *Seated left to right:* Thomas Eyre Booth, Harriet Emma "Hattie" Booth LeClere, Frank Walworth Booth. Courtesy of Helen Heckenlaible and Wilma Spice.

to study his life and accomplishments in depth. We know much less about the lives of these other deaf individuals.

ॐ§ॐ

AS A pioneer journalist on the Iowa frontier, Edmund lived an extraordinary life. His many writings portray the spirit and fortitude of a man who lived successfully in both the deaf and hearing communities of his time. He was one of the few deaf Americans of the nineteenth century who left behind a detailed and fascinating record of his thoughts and activities. His published works include articles in the *American Annals of the Deaf*, the *Annals of Iowa*, and decades of editorials in the *Anamosa Eureka* newspaper. His adventurous spirit, wise leadership, and ability to live in both the hearing and deaf worlds make him a prime subject for Disability Studies courses. He accepted the challenges of all kinds of obstacles and persevered, earning him great esteem by most people who interacted with him.

The Iowa community to which Edmund belonged thrived on this deaf man's literacy. For more than 50 years, he and his son Thomas brought the news of the world, local events, accounts of weddings, deaths of friends, and personal commentary into the homes of Jones County. His great intellect and sense of fairness earned him recognition as the patriarch of the American Deaf community. Thomas F. Fox, one of the founding members of the National Association of the Deaf, described Edmund as "a man of unusual intelligence and ability [who] presided over the opening proceedings with serene dignity, ever watchful that a strict regard for parliamentary order of procedure be observed."[4]

Mary Ann was also extraordinary. Although profoundly deaf and unable to speak intelligibly, she was far more literate than most frontierswomen with normal hearing. It is no overstatement to say that she played the most critical and supportive role in Edmund's success. She was more than a housewife and Edmund's "best friend," as she once put it. She provided the spiritual nourishment to the family. For five years while Edmund was in California, she raised two children, managed the family's financial affairs, and counseled him as they pursued their mutual destinies. She, too, left a remarkable legacy. Her own paper trail allows us to see in great detail the life of a deaf woman pioneer, and we remember her for her intelligence as well. She is the one who purchased the land for their home in Anamosa, a tract of land which became one of the busiest blocks in the town. She took the seeds from a tasty apple and planted them on that land, and the fruit from these trees was harvested for many years to come. When her young granddaughter Bertha died in May 1907, many full-blossomed branches from the tree that Mary Ann had nurtured from a seed, decorated the room where Bertha rested. She similarly created beauty in the spiritual life in her family. All three of the Booth children were active in church work throughout their lives. Thomas became a church deacon, Hattie married a minister, and Frank was a devoted churchgoer.

Edmund Booth knew what privation meant, but such insight was not at all a result of his deafness. His early years on the Iowa frontier and in the California gold mines were spent in communities where everyone was dependent on each other, and this experience shaped his perspectives on life. When he arrived at Buffalo Forks, Iowa, in 1839, there were no bridges built over any of the rivers. He saw the first telegraph and the first telephone come to Anamosa. Unlike many of his deaf contemporaries, for most of his life Edmund was not dependent upon a school for the deaf for his livelihood. He was a successful, self-made deaf man whose life choices were not dictated by a school administrator or board of directors, and he reveled in that freedom. His perseverance through all kinds of travails serves as an example for young people today, both hearing and deaf.

Despite the voluminous paper trail Edmund left us, unsolved mysteries about his life still remain. The first pertains to his treatment as a deaf man. The nineteenth century was a time of oppression of deaf people as well as women, African-Americans, and other marginalized groups. Yet, there is no mention in any letter, editorial, or other document handed down to us that indicates Edmund personally experienced negative treatment as a result of his deafness or his inability to speak clearly. He was harassed for his anti-slavery views; he engaged in intense debates with other deaf people about the formation of a Deaf commonwealth; and he became deeply involved in political battles with town officials and witty disputes with other newspaper editors. He traveled from coast to coast; mingled with Native

Americans, Mexicans, and various foreigners; conducted business with his mining, farming, and newspaper work; and corresponded with hundreds of people. But there is a complete absence of commentary by him regarding being mistreated as a deaf individual. Was this something he had learned to ignore? Did Edmund intimidate others with his powerful intellect, brawny physique, and ceaseless courage to undertake any challenge that confronted him? Or did he simply refuse to be thought of as a victim?

A second mystery relates to Edmund's private thoughts about his son Frank. The question that arises but probably can never be answered is, What were Edmund's true feelings about his son's zealous endorsement of the oral method of instruction? Clearly, Frank knew that sign language alone had no injurious effect on learning. Early communication between parents and deaf children and parental involvement in the child's development, as well as in fostering reading and writing skills, were acknowledged to be critically important to a child's success in school. All of these were emphases his father, a Renaissance man in that regard, had published on and commented on repeatedly through his life. Using sign language to communicate the most abstract ideas was indeed possible, and Frank had witnessed this firsthand in his family and in the families of his parents' deaf friends.

Perhaps, though, Frank made unfair comparisons between his father, a "semi-mute," and his mother, who depended on her children and others to give voice to her thoughts in daily interactions with hearing people. Frank also may have attributed his father's speaking skills to his independent, adventurous, and successful nature. While this may have been one factor, it is more likely that Frank saw the direction the field of deaf education was taking. Pennsylvania had recently passed legislation requiring oral education in its charter schools serving deaf children. At the time, there was little hope that the pendulum would swing back in support of sign language as a primary means of instruction. Frank thus may have adopted the oralist philosophy in order to advance himself among his peers.

In his weekly letters to his parents, Frank made it clear that he did not support the use of signed communication with young deaf children. Yet, despite his strong feelings about oralism for children, he still respected the use of sign language by adults. In a letter written in December 1896, he told his parents, "I am to go to the city this morning to court—to act as an interpreter for a deaf man."[5] In March 1897 he told his parents that he was lecturing [in sign] at a community meeting for deaf adults.

Although known for his extreme candor, Edmund seldom offered written comments of any kind regarding the career pursuits of his children. He may have harbored conflicting thoughts regarding oralism and the combined method (use of signs and spoken communication together), but he did not write to Frank about them. It is probable that, if mesmerism had worked, he and Mary Ann would have pursued it, and he would have sought a means for teaching Mary Ann to speak. Sign language was a powerful force in their lives, partly out of necessity, but certainly one of utmost value.

Edmund did write professionally about oral communication. In 1884, he published an article in the *American Annals of the Deaf and Dumb,* in which he admitted to never having been a good lipreader and having met only a few deaf people who possessed that skill.

> Leaving out those few who have a genius for lip-reading, is it not almost as absurd to expect the mass of deaf-mutes to acquire facility in that direction? . . . I do not object to teaching speech and lip-reading to those who have some degree of readiness at learning, but to doom them to that entirely, and to shut out the sign-language, by which, and almost alone, they can acquire ideas or the sense of words spoken, seems to me little else than an outrageous wrong. . . . Surely a system that thus forbids a knowledge of the sign-language to its pupils is *cruel.*[6]

Four years earlier, Edmund had written a less forceful article in the *American Annals* in which he argued that sign language provided the power to uninhibitedly express the mind and the heart and to foster mental development. In this 1880 article, published in the same year as the Milan Conference, he compared the early development of hearing and deaf children and noted that "signs constitute a natural mode of expression, and may enlarge in scope as new ideas and new objects make their presence known."[7]

Before Edmund died, Frank published papers with titles such as, "The Sign Language: Its Use and Abuse in the School-Room" (1883), "The Passing of the Sign Method" (1902), and "The Degeneracy of the Sign Language and Its Doom" (1905). He edited the journal published by Alexander Graham Bell's organization, the American Association to Promote the Teaching of Speech to the Deaf (AAPTSD). Through his editorials, he regularly expressed his alienation from the use of sign language in the schools, and he antagonized many in the American Deaf community. He received a salary for serving as general secretary and treasurer of the AAPTSD. He became intimate friends with Bell, who trusted him to promote the ideals of oralism. He mingled with such prominent oralists as Mary True, Carolyn Yale, and Gardiner Greene Hubbard, and he was called upon to join battles with the "Gallaudet factions" over communication methods used in individual schools.

Frank's biting editorials included a pronouncement in 1902 of the hope that "the sign method of instruction no longer exists anywhere nor is practiced in any school for the deaf in the world." Yet he acknowledged that for his own "entrance upon the work . . . [our life-long familiarity with sign language] was our principal recommendation and chief qualification. . . . we studied it, practiced it, and defended it upon occasion . . . with hardly a thought that there was any other method of educating the deaf worthy of the name."[8] He remained bitterly outspoken against the use of signs throughout his career. "The sign language is a weed language," he said in 1920. "It grows naturally and, if allowed to do so, it crowds out any and every other desirable growth. Now, we properly keep weeds out of the farm or the garden when we plant and cultivate things that we wish to grow. And that is what we must do in our schoolrooms where we are cultivating, developing the English language; we simply must keep the sign language out."[9] In his unabashed and paradoxical allegiance to the movement toward the dissolution of sign language, Frank may have trusted that his father was safely secluded by infirmity in his old age and too feeble to offer a final lesson on constructive discourse.

A third mystery about Edmund Booth concerns the fact that he was blind in one eye. As a profoundly deaf person myself, with many deaf friends, I wondered about this often while working on the book. The loss of vision is one of the biggest fears every deaf person experiences. Yet, this courageous frontiersman plowed his fields with rattlesnakes around, guarded his wagon train and later his mining camps after dark, and read and edited newspapers for decades without commenting on the challenges of his partial blindness. In fact, he made no mention of it at all until his waning years, when his remaining vision began to fail.

ॐৄৢৄ

THOMAS Eyre Booth died on April 5, 1927; Harriet Booth LeClere died on July 5, 1934; and Frank Walworth Booth died on March 21, 1938. However, several generations of Booth and Walworth descendants have followed closely the development of this book. Among them, in particular, is Thomas Eyre Booth's granddaughter, Helen Heckenlaible, who became a centenarian while this book was in process. Helen remembers that her grandfather often asked her to play a piano piece called "The Old Mill." Thomas would sit with a faraway look on his face, remembering the time long ago when he used to sit and fish from the old Metcalf grist mill, listening to the droning hum of the powerful water wheels, the "charming music" of his youthful days.

Such stories endure among the entire network of descendants of the Booth and Walworth families. The humanity and grace of Edmund and Mary Ann thus live on.

Notes

❧❦❧

Chapter 1. The Early Years

1. Edmund Booth, Autobiography, Private collection of Wilma Spice. Booth began to write his autobiography in 1885/1886, when he was 75 years old. He continued writing over a period of years and finally finished it sometime in 1898. Permission for all quotes from this autobiography has been granted by Wilma Spice, Edmund Booth's great-great-granddaughter.

2. Ibid., 8.

3. Ibid.

4. Ibid., 10, 8.

5. Ibid., 14.

6. Ibid.

7. This book will use "American Asylum," "Asylum," and "American School for the Deaf" interchangeably.

8. Margaret H. Hall, *The Aristocratic Journey; Being the Outspoken Letters of Mrs. Basil Hall Written during a Fourteen Months' Sojourn in America, 1827–1828* (New York: G. P. Putnam's Sons, 1931), 110.

9. E. Booth, Autobiography, 14–15.

10. Ibid., 15. Through much of his life, Edmund held an interest in phrenology, the study of mental capacity and character based on the structure of the human skull.

11. Edmund Booth, "Thomas Hopkins Gallaudet," *Iowa Hawkeye* (1881).

12. American School for the Deaf Archives, File "July 6 1829."

13. Edmund Booth, "Mr. Flournoy's Project," *American Annals of the Deaf and Dumb* 10 (1858): 73.

14. *Fifteenth Report of the Directors of the American Asylum at Hartford for the Education and Instruction of the Deaf and Dumb* (1831): 21.

15. *Fourteenth Report of the Directors of the American Asylum at Hartford for the Education and Instruction of the Deaf and Dumb* (1830): 28.

16. *Seventeenth Report of the Directors of the American Asylum at Hartford for the Education and Instruction of the Deaf and Dumb* (1833): 5–6.

17. See Harry G. Lang and William Stokoe, "A Treatise on Signed and Spoken Language in Early-19th-Century Deaf Education in America," *Journal of Deaf Studies and Deaf Education* 5 (2000): 196–216. Barnard had planned to have a legal career but changed his mind because of his hearing loss. His friends remembered that during his years at Yale his mood sometimes bordered on despair. Barnard's mother and brother were also deaf. At Hartford, Barnard focused on learning to sign and on developing his teaching philosophy. He was interested in the science of education, and this led him to systematically examine the communicative dimensions of instruction. He went on to have a distinguished career as a teacher and administrator at several universities; he served as president of Columbia College (now University) for 25 years.

18. Booth remembered Mary Ann's appearance at the school: "In this class of Barnard's and which I, still being a pupil, taught eight months, was the girl, Mary Ann Walworth, 14 years old, that, years later, became my wife" (Autobiography, 16).

19. E. Booth, Autobiography, 2.

20. Edmund Booth, "Miss Martineau and Deaf-Mutes," *American Annals of the Deaf and Dumb* 22 (1877): 81.

21. Lewis Weld to the President and Directors of the American Asylum, January 27, 1835. American School for the Deaf Archives.

22. E. Booth, Autobiography, 17.

23. See Phyllis Valentine, "Thomas Hopkins Gallaudet: Benevolent Paternalism and the Origins of the American Asylum," in *Deaf History Unveiled: Interpretations from the New Scholarship,* ed. John V. Van Cleve, 53–73 (Washington, DC: Gallaudet University Press, 1993).

24. E. Booth, Autobiography, 17.

Chapter 2. Journey to Iowa

1. E. Booth, Autobiography, 18.

2. Bertha Finn, Pat Worden Sutton, JoAnn McRoberts Walters, and Mildred Barker Brown, *Anamosa—1838–1938: A Reminiscence* (Monticello, IA: Monticello Express, 1988), 66.

3. E. Booth, Autobiography, 21.

4. Ibid., 21–22.

5. Ibid., 22–23.

6. Ibid., 26.

7. Ibid.

8. Ibid.

9. Emily's story is found in Thomas E. Booth, Reminiscences (ca. 1923), 6. Private collection of Wilma Spice.

Chapter 3. Anamosa

1. E. Booth, Autobiography, 27.

2. Ibid., 28–29.

3. Edmund Booth, "Early Education of Iowa Mutes," *Annals of Iowa* (1871): 686.

4. E. Booth, Autobiography, 29.

5. Booth made a claim west of the military road a mile south of what was later called Fairview. Then, it was known as "Russell's Place."

6. Edmund Booth, "Anamosa—Origin of Its Name," *Annals of Iowa* 12 (1874): 29.

7. Finn et al., *Anamosa 1838–1938*, 2, 69. Thus, it was in the framed house built by Edmund Booth, which became the Wapsipinicon Hotel, that the town's name—Anamosa—was born.

8. Edmund Booth to Mary Ann Booth, January 18, 1844. Hereafter, letters between Edmund and Mary Ann will be cited with the correspondents' initials.

9. Ibid.

10. Ibid.

11. Ibid.

12. Ibid.

13. E. Booth to M. A. Booth, February 6, 1844.

14. Ibid.

15. Ibid.

16. Ibid.

17. E. Booth to M. A. Booth, February 13, 1844.

18. Mary Ann wrote to Edmund on August 17, 1851, complaining about the mistreatment she suffered from Edmund's family. She said, "I think that they are worse than my own parents done [sic] to you when we lived with them in Illinois."

19. E. Booth to M. A. Booth, February 13, 1844.

20. Ibid.

21. Edmund Booth, "Reminiscences of Twenty-Seven Years Ago," *Annals of Iowa* 9 (1871): 564–65.

22. Ibid., 566.

23. Ibid., 567.

24. E. Booth to M. A. Booth, February 13, 1844.

25. It is not clear when Mary Ann and Thomas returned to Iowa. Edmund received a letter from Mary Ann, but he did not record the date.

26. This letter from Philura Walworth to Mary Ann, dated February 4, 1845, is found hand-copied in a letter from James Walworth to Mary Ann and Edmund Booth dated July 21, 1890. Courtesy of Dartmouth College Library.

27. E. Booth, Autobiography, 33.

28. Ibid. The first Harriet was born in Fairview on February 22, 1846, and died on July 31, 1847. The family looked for her grave years later but could not find it. They placed a small monument on the family plot in her memory.

29. E. Booth, Autobiography, 30–31.

30. T. E. Booth, Reminiscences, 7.

31. E. Booth, Autobiography, 34.

Chapter 4. On the California Trail

1. Benjamin Clough, "An Account of the Death of My Father," in *Thirteenth Report of the Directors of the American Asylum at Hartford for the Education and Instruction of the Deaf and Dumb* (1829): 31.

2. E. Booth to M. A. Booth, May 15, 1849. This letter was unsigned and addressed to Mary Ann Booth, Fairview, Jones County, Iowa. It was postmarked with a pen by the postmaster, "Newton, Iowa, Paid 5. May 23, 1849."

3. Ibid.

4. Ibid.

5. Ibid.

6. Ibid.

7. E. Booth to M. A. Booth, May 18, 1849.

8. E. Booth to M. A. Booth, May 21, 1849.

9. Ibid.

10. E. Booth, Autobiography, 35.

11. E. Booth to M. A. Booth, June 5, 1849.

12. E. Booth, Autobiography, 36, 37.

13. Fremont's book, first published in 1843, contained a summary of his early expeditions to California and Oregon. Many Forty-Niners took a copy with them as a guide.

14. E. Booth, Journal, August 1, 1849.

15. Ibid., August 4, 1849.

16. Ibid., August 9, 1849.

17. Ibid., August 24, 1849.

18. Ibid., September 5, 1849.

19. Ibid., September 10, 1849.

20. Ibid., September 11, 1849; September 12, 1849.
21. Ibid., September 14, 1849.
22. Ibid., September 23, 1849.
23. Ibid., September 25, 1849.
24. Ibid., September 26, 1849.
25. Ibid.
26. Ibid., September 27, 1849.
27. Ibid., October 1, 1849.
28. Ibid., October 13, 1849.
29. E. Booth, Autobiography, 34.

Chapter 5. The Making of a Forty-Niner

1. E. Booth, Autobiography, 40.
2. E. Booth to M. A. Booth, October 25, 1849.
3. Ibid.
4. E. Booth, Autobiography, 41.
5. Ibid., 42.
6. Ibid.
7. Ibid., 43.
8. Ibid., 44.
9. E. Booth to M. A. Booth, March 19, 1850.
10. E. Booth, Autobiography, 46.
11. M. A. Booth to E. Booth, January 3, 1850.
12. Ibid.
13. Ibid.
14. Not long afterwards, Edmund told Mary Ann that Clough had gone to the Middle Fork of the American River, where other miners had seen him. He was 50 miles away.
15. M. A. Booth to E. Booth, January 3, 1850.
16. E. Booth to M. A. Booth, March 19, 1850.
17. Ibid.
18. E. Booth to M. A. Booth, April 24, 1850.
19. E. Booth to M. A. Booth, August 18, 1850.
20. Edmund was wise with his investments. When another friend asked to borrow money at 4 percent interest a month to invest in sheep farming in San Diego, he declined this offer as well.
21. E. Booth to M. A. Booth, August 18, 1850.
22. Ibid.
23. E. Booth to M. A. Booth, August 19, 1850.

24. T. E. Booth, Reminiscences, 9–11.
25. E. Booth to M. A. Booth, September 1, 1850.
26. Ibid.
27. Ibid.
28. Ibid.
29. Ibid.
30. Ibid.
31. E. Booth to M. A. Booth, November 3, 1850.
32. Ibid.
33. Ibid.
34. Ibid.
35. Ibid.
36. E. Booth, Autobiography, 47.
37. E. Booth to M. A. Booth, November 3, 1850.
38. Ibid.

Chapter 6. Best Friends

1. E. Booth to M. A. Booth, January 20, 1851.
2. Ibid.
3. Ibid.
4. Ibid.
5. Ibid.
6. Ibid.
7. E. Booth to M. A. Booth, January 24, 1851.
8. Ibid.
9. Ibid.
10. E. Booth to M. A. Booth, February 6, 1851.
11. Ibid.
12. M. A. Booth to E. Booth, April 3, 1851.
13. Ibid.
14. Ibid.
15. Ibid.
16. Ibid.
17. Ibid.
18. Ibid.
19. E. Booth to M. A. Booth, April 27, 1851.
20. Ibid.
21. Ibid.
22. Ibid.

23. Within a short time, the *Courier*, which he considered the best paper in California, started up again, much to his relief.

24. E. Booth to M. A. Booth, June 8, 1851.

25. Ibid.

26. Ibid.

27. Ibid.

28. Ibid.

29. M. A. Booth to E. Booth, August 17, 1851.

30. T. E. Booth, Reminiscences, 4.

31. M. A. Booth to E. Booth, August 17, 1851.

32. Ibid.

33. Ibid.

34. Ibid.

35. Harriet Booth LeClere, Reminiscences (ca. 1923), 1. Private collection of Wilma Spice.

36. E. Booth to M. A. Booth, September 28, 1851.

37. E. Booth to M. A. Booth, October 5, 1851.

38. M. A. Booth to E. Booth, October 19, 1851.

39. Ibid.

40. T. E. Booth, Reminiscences, 4.

41. Ibid.

42. Ibid., 8.

43. M. A. Booth to E. Booth, October 19, 1851.

44. T. E. Booth, Reminiscences, 19.

45. M. A. Booth to E. Booth, October 19, 1851.

46. Ibid.

47. E. Booth to T. E. Booth, December 4, 1851.

48. E. Booth to M. A. Booth, December 5, 1851.

49. E. Booth to T. E. Booth, December 5, 1851.

50. E. Booth to T. E. Booth, December 7, 1851.

51. E. Booth to M. A. Booth, December 7, 1851.

52. Ibid.

53. E. Booth to M. A. Booth, December 21, 1851.

54. Ibid.

55. Ibid.

56. Ibid.

Chapter 7. Wearing Out

1. E. Booth to M. A. Booth, January 21, 1852.

2. Ibid.

3. Ibid.
4. T. E. Booth to E. Booth, undated, probably February 16, 1852.
5. Ibid.
6. M. A. Booth to E. Booth, March 15, 1852.
7. Ibid.
8. Ibid.
9. Ibid.
10. E. Booth to M. A. Booth, April 10, 1852.
11. Ibid.
12. E. Booth to M. A. Booth, April 24, 1852.
13. Ibid.
14. Ibid.
15. M. A. Booth to E. Booth, May 2, 1852.
16. Ibid.
17. T. E. Booth to his granddaughter, Helen Heckenlaible, April 7, 1913.
18. E. Booth to M. A. Booth, May 25, 1852.
19. Ibid.
20. Ibid.
21. Ibid.
22. Ibid.
23. E. Booth to M. A. Booth, July 11, 1852.
24. Ibid.
25. Ibid.
26. E. Booth to M. A. Booth, August 8, 1852.
27. E. Booth to M. A. Booth, August 12, 1852.
28. E. Booth to M. A. Booth, August 26, 1852.
29. M. A. Booth to E. Booth, November 9, 1852.
30. Ibid.
31. Ibid.
32. E. Booth to M. A. Booth, January 8, 1853.
33. E. Booth to M. A. Booth, January 10, 1853.
34. M. A. Booth to E. Booth, March 19, 1853.
35. E. Booth to M. A. Booth, April 10, 1853.
36. Ibid.
37. Ibid.
38. E. Booth to T. E. Booth, April 16, 1853.
39. M. A. Booth to E. Booth, July 22, 1853.
40. Ibid.
41. Ibid.
42. E. Booth to M. A. Booth, September 24, 1853.

43. E. Booth to M. A. Booth, November 13, 1853.
44. E. Booth, Autobiography, 49.

Chapter 8. Home Again

1. E. Booth, Autobiography, 51.
2. Ibid.
3. Ibid., 52.
4. T. E. Booth, Reminiscences, 2.
5. H. B. LeClere, Reminiscences, 1.
6. T. E. Booth, Reminiscences, 3.
7. H. B. LeClere, Reminiscences, 1.
8. E. Booth, Autobiography, 17.
9. T. E. Booth, Reminiscences, 23.
10. Ibid.
11. Ibid., 8.
12. Ibid., 17.
13. In March 1860, the first train entered the Anamosa depot, where a large contingent of townsfolk celebrated its arrival.
14. T. E. Booth, Reminiscences, 22.
15. Ibid., 30.
16. The building stood unfinished for three years while Green's estate was settled. William T. Shaw bought the building and added the finishing touches to it. J. H. Fisher and Son acquired it after that, then P. M. Wallace bought the building for a bakery.
17. *Anamosa Eureka*, January 28, 1859.
18. *Anamosa Eureka*, February 25, 1859.
19. *Anamosa Eureka*, April 15, 1859.
20. This poem was reprinted in the *Anamosa Eureka*, April 6, 1905, following Edmund's death.
21. *Anamosa Eureka*, June 17, 1859, 2.

Chapter 9. The Civil War Years

1. Wendell Phillips, *Speeches, Lectures, and Letters* (Boston: James Redpath, 1863), 1–10.
2. *Anamosa Eureka*, December 28, 1860, 2.
3. Ibid.
4. *Anamosa Eureka*, February 15, 1861, 2.
5. *Anamosa Eureka*, April 26, 1861, 2.

6. *Anamosa Eureka*, May 31, 1861, 2.

7. *Anamosa Eureka*, August 2, 1861, 2.

8. *Anamosa Eureka*, August 9, 1861, 2.

9. *Anamosa Eureka*, August 16, 1861, 2.

10. *Anamosa Eureka*, August 23, 1861, 2.

11. *Anamosa Eureka*, March 28, 1862, 1.

12. *Anamosa Eureka*, July 17, 1863, 1.

13. *Anamosa Eureka*, July 10, 1863, 2.

14. T. E. Booth, Reminiscences, 33.

15. E. Booth to M. A. Booth, February 13, 1844.

16. T. E. Booth, Reminiscences, 34.

17. Ibid.

18. *Anamosa Eureka*, May 17, 1861, 2.

19. H. B. LeClere, Reminiscences, 3.

20. *Anamosa Eureka*, June 5, 1863, 2.

21. T. E. Booth, Reminiscences, 31.

22. H. B. LeClere, Reminiscences, 3.

23. William Lloyd Garrison, preface to *Narrative of the Life of Frederick Douglass, an American Slave,* by Frederick Douglass (Boston: Anti-Slavery Office, 1845).

24. *Anamosa Eureka*, February 23, 1865, 2.

25. *Anamosa Eureka*, March 30, 1865, 2.

26. *Anamosa Eureka*, April 13, 1865, 2.

27. *Anamosa Eureka*, April 20, 1865, 2.

28. H. B. LeClere, Reminiscences, 3.

Chapter 10. Raising a Family

1. *Anamosa Eureka*, March 23, 1865, 3.

2. *Anamosa Eureka*, January 25, 1866, 2.

3. This monument was not completed until 1910.

4. H. B. LeClere, Reminiscences, 4.

5. Ibid, 5.

6. M. A. Booth to E. Booth, July 19, 1868. Courtesy of Dartmouth College Library.

7. Ibid.

8. Ibid.

9. After Thomas and Gertrude moved out, other tenants lived in the house. Early one morning in 1881, the house burned down.

10. T. E. Booth, Reminiscences, 27.

11. Ibid., 29.

12. E. Booth to F. W. Booth, April 30, 1873. Courtesy of Dartmouth College Library.

13. *Anamosa Eureka*, October 24, 1867, 3.

14. Finn et al., *Anamosa 1838–1938*, 47.

15. *Anamosa Eureka*, August 10, 1871, 3.

16. *Anamosa Eureka*, July 20, 1871, 3.

17. *Anamosa Eureka*, August 27, 1868, 3.

18. *Anamosa Eureka*, March 28, 1867, 3.

19. T. E. Booth, Reminiscences, 3.

20. *Anamosa Eureka*, May 16, 1867, 2.

21. *Anamosa Eureka*, February 11, 1869, 3.

22. *Anamosa Eureka*, February 8, 1872, 2.

23. *Anamosa Eureka*, May 2, 1872, 2.

24. *Anamosa Eureka*, February 18, 1869, 2.

Chapter 11. The Deaf Community

1. Edwin Isaac Holycross, *The Abbé de l'Epée, Founder of the Manual Instruction of the Deaf, and Other Early Teachers of the Deaf* (Columbus, OH: Holycross, 1913), 66.

2. "Philadelphia, Pa.," *The Silent Worker* 13 (May 1901): 131.

3. James F. Brady, "Inanities," *The Silent Worker* 37 (April 1925): 330; "The Temple of Fame," *The Silent Worker* 32 (November 1918): 24.

4. Edmund Booth, "On Emigration to the West by Deaf Mutes," *American Annals of the Deaf and Dumb* 10 (1858): 47.

5. *Anamosa Eureka*, May 10, 1858.

6. *Anamosa Eureka*, July 15, 1869, 3.

7. *Anamosa Eureka*, February 5, 1869, 2.

8. *Anamosa Eureka*, December 10, 1868, 2.

9. *Anamosa Eureka*, February 18, 1869, 1.

10. Edmund Booth, "Early Education of Iowa Mutes." *Annals of Iowa* 9 (1871): 690.

11. Ibid., 690–91.

12. Ibid., 691.

13. Ibid., 692.

14. Ibid.

15. John V. Van Cleve and Barry A. Crouch, *A Place of Their Own* (Washington, DC: Gallaudet University Press, 1989), 61.

16. William W. Turner to John J. Flournoy, reprinted in "Scheme for a Commonwealth of the Deaf and Dumb," *American Annals of the Deaf and Dumb* 8 (January 1856): 118–19.

17. Guilbert C. Braddock, "John Jacobus Flournoy," in *Notable Deaf Persons* (Washington, DC: Gallaudet College Alumni Association, 1975), 10.

18. Edmund Booth, "Mr. Booth to Mr. Flournoy," *American Annals of the Deaf and Dumb* 10 (1858): 41.

19. Ibid., 42

20. John J. Flournoy, "Mr. Flournoy to Mr. Turner," *American Annals of the Deaf and Dumb* 10 (1858): 45.

21. Edmund Booth, "Mr. Flournoy's Project," *American Annals of the Deaf and Dumb* 10 (1858): 74–75.

22. *Seventeenth Report of the Directors of the American Asylum at Hartford for the Education and Instruction of the Deaf and Dumb* (Hartford: Hudson and Skinner Printers, 1833), 33.

23. For a detailed analysis of the commonwealth debate, see B. A. Crouch, "Alienation and the Mid-Nineteenth Century American Deaf Community: A Response," *American Annals of the Deaf* 131 (1986): 322–24; and Van Cleve and Crouch, *A Place of Their Own,* 60–69.

24. Edmund Booth, "Remarks by Mr. Booth," *American Annals of the Deaf and Dumb* 10 (1858): 152, 154.

25. Van Cleve and Crouch, *A Place of Their Own,* 18.

26. "A Silent Commencement," *Anamosa Eureka,* August 5, 1869, 1.

27. See Van Cleve and Crouch, *A Place of Their Own,* 106–27, for an explanation of the methods controversy.

28. "An Honored Nestor," *The Silent Worker,* 13 (May 1901): 136. These comments were written by a teacher who had been at the Pennsylvania Institution at the time of Edmund's first visit in 1876.

29. Edmund Booth, "Miss Martineau and Deaf-Mutes," *American Annals of the Deaf and Dumb* 22 (1877): 83.

30. *American Annals of the Deaf and Dumb* 25 (1880): 85.

31. *American Annals of the Deaf and Dumb* 26 (1881): 172.

32. See Van Cleve and Crouch, *A Place of Their Own,* 109–110.

33. A. A. Kinsey, *Report of the Proceedings of the International Congress on the Education of the Deaf* (London: W. H. Allen, 1880).

34. *Association Review,* 3 (1901): 149, 151.

35. H. B. LeClere, Reminiscences, 3.

36. *Twenty-third Annual Report of the Columbia Institution for the Deaf and Dumb for the Fiscal Year Ending June 30, 1880* (Washington, DC: Government Printing Office, 1880).

37. George Veditz, "The Genesis of the National Association," *Deaf Mutes'
Journal* 62 (June 1, 1933): 1.

38. Ibid.

39. "Edmund Booth," *The Silent Worker* 17 (May 1905): 123.

40. *Proceedings of the First National Convention of Deaf-Mutes held in Cincinnati, Ohio*, August 26–28, 1880, 1.

41. Ibid., 26.

42. Ibid., 27.

43. See Van Cleve and Crouch, *A Place of Their Own*, 93–94.

44. Veditz, *Deaf Mutes' Journal*, 1.

45. Ibid.

46. Edmund Booth, "Classifying Words," *American Annals of the Deaf and Dumb* 25 (1880): 126. The sign for "president" is still used today, but the sign for "governor" has changed. The evolution of signs has accelerated considerably since Booth's time.

47. Ibid., 127–28.

48. W. H. Gemmil, "Edmund Booth, 1810–1905." Address delivered at the Eighteenth Convention of the Iowa Association of the Deaf, August 20, 1931.

49. F. W. Booth to E. Booth and M. A. Booth, February 21, 1886. Courtesy of Dartmouth College Library.

50. F. W. Booth to E. Booth and M. A. Booth, October 27, 1889. Courtesy of Dartmouth College Library.

Chapter 12: The Sound of Trumpets

1. Harriet and George LeClere's children were Laura Booth LeClere, born July 12, 1876; Edmund George LeClere, born May 6, 1878; Emily Garfield LeClere, born December 20, 1880; Frank Walworth LeClere, born March 9, 1883; Herbert Laude LeClere, born August 1, 1885; Mary Louise LeClere, born December 8, 1886, and Walter Booth LeClere, born May 31, 1890. Frank and Marion Booth's children were Edmund Hendershot Booth, born October 25, 1895; Marion Frances Booth, born May 13, 1898; and Robert Plues Booth, born August 16, 1900.

2. H. B. LeClere, Reminiscences, 5–6.

3. C. S. Millard, "Reminiscences," *Anamosa Eureka*, April 20, 1905.

4. J. J. Walworth to M. A. and E. Booth, July 21, 1890. Courtesy of Dartmouth College Library.

5. Ibid.

6. Ibid.

7. Ibid.

8. T. E. Booth, Reminiscences, 28.

9. F. W. Booth to E. Booth and M. A. Booth, March 26, 1893. Courtesy of Dartmouth College Library.

10. Ibid.

11. F. W. Booth to E. Booth and M. A. Booth, May 14, 1893. Courtesy of Dartmouth College Library.

12. J. J. Walworth to M. A. Booth, May 1895. Courtesy of Dartmouth College Library.

13. F. W. Booth to E. Booth and M. A. Booth, February 3, 1896. Courtesy of Dartmouth College Library.

14. F. W. Booth to E. Booth and M. A. Booth, March 1, 1897. Courtesy of Dartmouth College Library.

15. F. W. Booth to E. Booth and M. A. Booth, October 18, 1897. Courtesy of Dartmouth College Library.

16. On February 3, 1898, the *Eureka* carried a summary of Mary Ann Walworth Booth's funeral, including Rev. Millikan's eulogy and her life history. Mary Ann was survived by her brother, James J. Walworth of Boston, and by two sisters, Emily (Mrs. Rev. L. B. Fifield) of Minneapolis, Minnesota, and Caroline (Mrs. Rev. Dr. D. T. Fiske) of Newburyport, Massachusetts.

17. Ibid.

18. Ibid.

19. H. B. LeClere, Reminiscences, 4.

20. *Anamosa Eureka*, February 3, 1898.

21. E. Booth, Autobiography, 52.

22. E. Booth to F. W. and M. H. Booth, March 13, 1898. Courtesy of Dartmouth College Library.

23. *Anamosa Eureka*, July 23, 1931, 1.

24. T. E. Booth, Reminiscences, 32.

25. "Philadelphia, Pa.," *The Silent Worker* 13 (May 1901): 131.

26. T. E. Booth, Reminiscences, 18.

27. E. Booth, Autobiography, 42.

28. T. E. Booth, Reminiscences, 36.

29. *Deaf Mutes' Journal* 62 (June 1, 1933): 1.

30. T. E. Booth, Reminiscences, 18.

31. Reprinted in the *Anamosa Eureka*, August 25, 1904.

32. *Anamosa Eureka*, April 6, 1905.

33. Ibid.

34. J. N. Davidson to T. E. Booth, April 8, 1905.

35. *Proceedings of the Seventeenth Meeting of the Convention of American Instructors of the Deaf* (Washington, DC: Government Printing Office, 1906), 175.

36. Reprinted in the *Anamosa Eureka*, April 6, 1905.

Afterword

1. C. S. Millard, "Reminiscences." *Anamosa Eureka*, April 20, 1905.

2. Nancy Rowe Curtis Papers, University of Michigan.

3. E. Booth, Autobiography, 49.

4. *The Iowa Hawkeye*, October 15, 1931, 4.

5. F. W. Booth to E. Booth and M. A. Booth, December 28, 1896. Courtesy of Dartmouth College Library.

6. Edmund Booth, "A Genius for Lip-Reading," *American Annals of the Deaf and Dumb* 29 (1884): 20–21.

7. Edmund Booth, "Classifying Words," *American Annals of the Deaf and Dumb* 25 (1880): 126.

8. Frank W. Booth, "The Passing of the Sign Method," *Association Review* 4 (1902): 190, 188.

9. Frank's comments were printed in Elbert A. Gruver, "Training of Backward Deaf Children," in *Proceedings of the Twenty-second Meeting of the Joint Convention of American Instructors of the Deaf* (Washington, DC: Government Printing Office, 1921), 231.

Bibliography

Writings of Edmund Booth

1829 "Invasion of Greece by Persians." In *Thirteenth Report of the Directors of the American Asylum at Hartford for the Education and Instruction of the Deaf and Dumb.*

1830 "Heavenly Bodies." In *Fourteenth Report of the Directors of the American Asylum at Hartford for the Education and Instruction of the Deaf and Dumb.*

1831 "Dialogue Between a Greek Patriot and an Educated American Deaf and Dumb Man. In *Fifteenth Report of the Directors of the American Asylum at Hartford for the Education and Instruction of the Deaf and Dumb.*

1832 "On the Present State of European Governments." In *Sixteenth Report of the Directors of the American Asylum at Hartford for the Education and Instruction of the Deaf and Dumb.*

1833 "On Education in the United States." In *Seventeenth Report of the Directors of the American Asylum at Hartford for the Education and Instruction of the Deaf and Dumb.*

1834 "Soliloquy of Bonaparte on His Voyage to St. Helena." In *Eighteenth Report of the Directors of the American Asylum at Hartford for the Education and Instruction of the Deaf and Dumb.*

1858 "Mr. Booth to Mr. Flournoy." *American Annals of the Deaf and Dumb* 10: 40–42.

"Mr. Flournoy's Project." *American Annals of the Deaf and Dumb* 10: 72–79.

"On Emigration to the West by Deaf Mutes." *American Annals of the Deaf and Dumb* 10: 46–51.

"Remarks by Mr. Booth." *American Annals of the Deaf and Dumb* 10: 151–54.

1859 "On Emigration of Deaf-Mutes to the West." *American Annals of the Deaf and Dumb* 11: 160–63.

1871 "Reminiscences of Twenty-seven Years Ago." *Annals of Iowa* 9: 562–67.

"Early Education of Iowa Mutes." *Annals of Iowa* 9: 684–93.

1874 "Anamosa—Origin of Its Name." *Annals of Iowa* 12: 27–31.

1877 "Miss Martineau and Deaf Mutes." *American Annals of the Deaf and Dumb* 22: 80–83.

1878 "Punctuation as an Aid in the Education of Deaf-Mutes." *American Annals of the Deaf and Dumb* 23: 72–83.

1880 "Classifying Words." *American Annals of the Deaf and Dumb* 25: 126–35.

1881 "Thomas Hopkins Gallaudet." *Iowa Hawkeye.* Reprinted in the *North Dakota Banner* 53 (December 1943): 1–2.

1884 "A Genius for Lip-Reading," *American Annals of the Deaf and Dumb* 29: 17–21.

1885 "Punctuation." *American Annals of the Deaf and Dumb* 30: 204–11.

1890 Autobiography. Private collection of Wilma Spice.

Other Works Cited

Booth, Frank W. "Edmund Booth: A Life Sketch." *Association Review* 7 (1905): 225–37.

Booth, Thomas E. Reminiscences (ca. 1923). Private collection of Helen Heckenlaible and Wilma Spice.

Braddock, Guilbert. *Notable Deaf Persons.* Washington, DC: Gallaudet College Alumni Association, 1975.

Edmund Booth, Forty-Niner: The Life Story of a Deaf Pioneer. Stockton, CA: San Joaquin Pioneer and Historical Society, 1953.

"Edmund Booth: Founder of the NAD." *The Silent Worker* 15 (January 1963): 6.

Fay, Edward A. "Edmund Booth." *American Annals of the Deaf* 50 (1905): 320–21.

Finn, Bertha, Pat Worden Sutton, JoAnn McRoberts Walters, and Mildred Barker Brown. *Anamosa—1838–1938: A Reminiscence.* Monticello, IA: Monticello Express, 1988.

Gallaher, James E., ed. *Representative Deaf Persons of the United States of America.* Chicago: J. E. Gallaher, 1898.

"God's Finger Touched Him and He Slept." Obituary of Edmund Booth. *Anamosa Eureka,* April 6, 1905.

Haise, R. "Letters from the People." *Stockton* (California) *Record,* October 14, 1953.

Heckenlaible, Helen A. Review of *Edmund Booth, Forty-Niner. California Herald,* November 1954, 7.

———. *Autobiography and Family History of Helen Adele Brewer Heckenlaible.* Pittsburgh, PA: privately printed, 2001.

Hendricks, Jill, and John V. Van Cleve. "Edmund and Mary Ann Walworth Booth." Paper presented at the Deaf History International Conference, Trondheim, Norway, September 1997.

History of Jones County, Iowa, Containing a History of the County, Its Cities, Towns, Etc., Biographical Sketches of Citizens. Chicago: Western Historical Co., 1879.

Holycross, Edwin I. *The Abbé De l'Epée (Charles Michel De L'Epée), Founder of the Manual Instruction of the Deaf, and Other Early Teachers of the Deaf.* Columbus, OH: Edwin Isaac Holycross, 1913.

Jackson, J. H. "Between the Lines." *San Francisco Chronicle,* December 20, 1953.

Lang, Harry G., and Bonnie Meath-Lang. "Edmund Booth." In *Deaf Persons in the Arts and Sciences: A Biographical Dictionary,* 45–47. Westport, CT: Greenwood Press, 1995.

LeClere, Harriet Booth. Reminiscences (ca. 1923). Private collection of Helen Heckenlaible and Wilma Spice.

Van Cleve, John.V. "Edmund Booth." In *Gallaudet Encyclopedia of Deaf People and Deafness,* edited by John V. Van Cleve, 143–44. New York: McGraw-Hill, 1987.

Valentine, Phyllis. "Thomas Hopkins Gallaudet: Benevolent Paternalism and the Origins of the American Asylum." In *Deaf History Unveiled: Interpretations from the New Scholarship,* edited by John V. Van Cleve, 53–73. Washington, DC: Gallaudet University Press, 1993.

Index

Numbers in italics indicate photographs.